GEORGE WASHINGTON
AND THE IRISH

GEORGE WASHINGTON AND THE IRISH

Incredible Stories of the Irish Spies, Soldiers, and Workers Who Helped Free America

Niall O'Dowd

Skyhorse Publishing

Skyhorse Publishing books may be purchased in bulk at special discounts for sales promotion, corporate gifts, fund-raising, or educational purposes. Special editions can also be created to specifications. For details, contact the Special Sales Department, Skyhorse Publishing, 307 West 36th Street, 11th Floor, New York, NY 10018 or info@skyhorsepublishing.com.

Skyhorse® and Skyhorse Publishing® are registered trademarks of Skyhorse Publishing, Inc.®, a Delaware corporation.

Visit our website at www.skyhorsepublishing.com.

10 9 8 7 6 5 4 3 2 1

Library of Congress Cataloging-in-Publication Data is available on file.

Cover design by Kai Texel

Print ISBN: 978-1-5107-6939-7
Ebook ISBN: 978-1-5107-6940-3

Printed in the United States of America

This Book is Dedicated to All Those Who Fight for Freedom

CONTENTS

ACKNOWLEDGMENTS

This book became an obvious undertaking after the very successful *Lincoln and the Irish: The Untold Story of How the Irish Helped Abraham Lincoln Save the Union*, which was published in March 2018.

Researching the Irish and Washington was a fascinating undertaking. I learned so much about the close ties that bound him to his Irish followers.

Washington and Lincoln stand apart in American history, yet the role the Irish played in their success has been massively ignored.

One does not have to exaggerate or overplay the Irish role in either case; we can let their words and deeds speak for themselves. It is also a fact that the Irish story and their part in the American Revolution needs to be told.

My sincere thanks to Tony Lyons, president and publisher at Skyhorse Publishing, for his support in launching this Washington book, and to his excellent editor and advisor Caroline Russomanno for her insights and support.

A special thanks to Darina Molloy, who did such a fine editing job on the original manuscript and correcting my strange reluctance to admit that commas do exist.

Finally to my wife Debbie, a great journalist who advised and supported at every turn, and also to my daughter Alana for her heartfelt support and encouragement.

Thank you all.

Go N-Eiri Libh. Success to all.

—Niall O'Dowd
October 2021

"*America was lost by Irish emigrants . . . I am assured from the best authority, the major part of the American Army was composed of Irish and that the Irish language was as commonly spoken in the American ranks as English, I am also informed it was their valor that determined the contest . . .* "
Lord Mountjoy, British Parliament, April 2, 1784

Freedom's Sons and Daughters— The Story of the Irish and George Washington

There is no doubt that Ireland's sons and daughters played a major role in the battle for American independence from the British Crown.

As leading Revolutionary War historian Thomas Fleming has noted, the Irish "responded en masse to the call for resistance to England. With more than 300,000 of them in the colonies, they had a major impact on the war."

You would be hard-pressed to find an account of the full Irish commitment. Historians have mainly ignored or rarely referenced their role. This is an opportunity to set the record straight.

As Philip Thomas Tucker, PhD, a prolific historian of the Revolutionary War writes: "For more than two centuries, what has been most forgotten about America's stirring creation story were the crucial and disproportionate contributions that the Irish people played in the winning of the American Revolution."

What this book shows is that the impact of the Irish was not confined to war: it was the loving care given by Irish nurses to wounded soldiers; it was the cooking, cleaning, and laundry work done by Irish camp followers that kept an army marching; it was

the fearless advocacy for freedom from successful immigrant politicians and business leaders; it was the secret intelligence and spy
work that resulted in great victories and disasters avoided. And yes,
of course, there was the bravery of the men who fought at Bunker
Hill, Princeton, Trenton, Yorktown, and all the great battle sites.

There is the closeness of Washington to the Irish, rarely revealed.

We will also see the social Washington—a beloved and frequent
guest at the Friendly Sons of Saint Patrick's dinners or visiting with
his favorite Irish bartender in a Delaware Irish pub. We will see him
during formal occasions—dancing minuets and waltzes at the home
of his great Irish friend General Henry Knox or wining and dining
his Irish neighbors at Mount Vernon.

Of course, there was the famous Saint Patrick's Day celebration
in 1780 after a winter of discontent at Valley Forge, but there is also
the story of how the Irish and German soldiers almost came to blows
as Washington tried to intervene. The following year, Washington
used Saint Patrick's Day as the only day off of the year to uplift his
men after a cruel winter.

It was an almost mystical bond between Washington and the
Irish: the fierce commitment when they realized Washington was not
anti-Irish Catholic like so many and was ready to die for his ideals;
and the fact that he hated the common enemy, the British, as much
as they did.

Indeed, in one case, we find Washington marveling at the ornate
statuary at a Catholic mass he attended and wondering why he
wasn't more drawn to the religion.

Battlefield generals and ordinary soldiers fought with rare fury
for him. The obscure tailor Hercules Mulligan became a master spy,
one so good that CIA Chief William Casey once wondered if he
wasn't the greatest American spy of all. Mary Travers, a beloved
nurse, became an angel of the camps. Elizabeth Thompson became
Washington's housekeeper at the age of seventy-two, and he was
devoted to her.

There is also the story of men like Washington's Chief Aide John
Fitzgerald whose riveting account of crossing the Delaware with

Washington provided an incredible eyewitness account of perhaps the most important moment in America's history.

George Washington and the Irish will show the bravery of the Irishmen who knew they could be signing their death warrants when they printed and signed the Declaration of Independence. For many, it was revenge for what the British had done to them in their own country.

We will also highlight the story of James Hoban, the unknown Irish architect who had a chance encounter with Washington and ended up designing the White House.

This book, then, is the largely untold story of how the Irish played a decisive part in helping George Washington defeat the British in perhaps the most significant war in history—a war where democracy was first forged and the divine right of kings to rule was forever ended. It also dispels the myths that few Irish Catholics fought. There were ten thousand Irish names on the Continental Army muster rolls at the beginning of the war and many more joined.

There were also, of course, thousands of Scots Irish Presbyterians, themselves forced to leave Ireland because of the draconian Penal Laws that forbid any religion but Anglican, also known as the Church of England. Among those who fought were the teenage son of Irish immigrants, Andrew Jackson, and Kate Barry, daughter of Irish immigrants, who became a legendary figure.

We will relay the extraordinary experiences of ordinary people at the time, witnesses to history like the Irish man who took care of Benjamin Franklin in his later years and who witnessed the final embrace between Washington and Franklin. We will also read Franklin's prescient letter from Ireland.

There is also the extraordinary tale of how the iconic Washington painting we are all so familiar with, the one used on the one dollar bill, was first dreamt up by a prisoner in an Irish debtor's jail.

We also have an Irish rogue's gallery with these pages, including the Irish major general who was the leader in a plot to see Washington replaced and possibly eliminated after early losses. The first traitor in American history to be hanged was Irish, as well.

The scope of *George Washington and the Irish* covers the numerous generals and lieutenants from Ireland that Washington had under his command and his complete familiarity with the Irish situation, which he likened to Americans trying to roust the British.

He could hardly have been unaware of the importance of the Irish to him. According to Christopher Klein, writing on History. com: "Generals born in Ireland or who had Irish parents commanded seven of the eleven brigades wintering in Morristown."

So this book covers the Revolutionary War contributions of ordinary men and women who never wrote down their history and involvement in events—many indeed were illiterate to begin with. Those who wrote the history hardly bothered with the immigrants, anyway; they were viewed by most with a severely jaundiced eye. Many were indentured servants essentially owned by their masters until they paid them back for their passage to America.

So the stories of how the Irish fought for, died for, bled for, and won massive naval battles for George Washington are generally untold, as is the story of the Cork soldier who first referred to the "United States of America." The heroism of the Scots Irish in the war is also revealed.

There are, also, extraordinarily uplifting stories.

When Washington was elected president, the Continental Congress sent an Irishman from Derry, Charles Thomson, the secretary of the Congress (in essence the speaker), to inform him. The fact that Thomson had arrived in America as a penniless orphan makes his story all the more remarkable.

We will also deal with the issue of slavery and the Irish, and the sad realization that many Irish, despite their own background of oppression, were sadly lacking any insight into how dreadful slavery was, though there were many honorable exceptions.

Charles Thomson, for instance, did more than free slaves; he hired Black labor and allowed them to work their own shareholding lands and provided decent accommodation for them.

Twelve American presidents owned slaves, which, alas, was the wretched context of the times, but many of the Irish seemed indifferent to the awful mistreatment of slaves.

The military contribution has long been omitted but that is changing. As historian Phillip Thomas Tucker puts it: "So many Irish served in the ranks of the Pennsylvania Continental Line, the backbone of Washington's Continental Army and one [of] its largest units, that this hard-fighting unit was correctly known as the 'Line of Ireland.'"

We have the singular testimony of the famed Virginia cavalry-man "Light Horse Harry" Lee (father of Robert E. Lee) who said the Irish line was "singularly fitted for close and stubborn action, hand to hand, in the center of the army, and always preferred an appeal to the bayonet to a toilsome march." Another officer said of them: "[T]hey served everywhere and surrendered nowhere."

* * *

Historian Michael O'Brien, after exhaustive research, reckoned 38 percent of Washington's Army was Irish or Scots Irish. O'Brien produced evidence from Revolutionary muster rolls that there were 695 Kellys in the American army, 494 Murphys, 331 McCarthys, 327 Connors or O'Connors, 322 Ryans, and 248 Doughertys—and that was before other common names were counted.

Yet the Irish have been shut out of Revolutionary War history as it has been written by grandees who had no time for the immigrants and their spawn. Anti-Catholicism ran rampant but there never was a harsh word on a person's religion from Washington, it must be noted.

As historian Thomas Fleming notes: "Henry Cabot Lodge tried to claim that the revolutionaries in Massachusetts were 'of almost pure English blood, with a small infusion of Scotch Irish from Londonderry.'" Actually, Historian O'Brien found three thousand unquestionably Irish names on the state's revolutionary muster rolls—and not one Lodge.

So the numbers speak for themselves. The glorious chapter of the Irish in the fight for democracy has never been fully told. This book is not an exhaustive "who's who" of everyone who fought or led (or it would be as long as the bible) but an overdue account of the importance of Erin's sons and daughters in achieving that most vital of victories. It also highlights the rarely revealed unbreakable link between Washington and his Irish comrades; something, ironically, the British grasped as Lord Mountjoy's quote that opened the book shows.

On far foreign fields, the soldiers and chiefs of the Irish brigades fought and died, but their contribution was never greater than helping create the dawn of democracy. Born into oppression, they became freedom's sons and daughters.

A Fine Day for Freedom

On Evacuation Day in New York, November 25, 1783, before George Washington arrived to declare his country free, the last skirmish of the Revolutionary War that changed the world forever occurred.

It involved a proud newly-minted American citizen, whose first name is lost to history, the wife of Irish American Benjamin Day, and an outraged British officer on Murray Street, now part of the district known as Tribeca in Manhattan.

Mrs. Day kept a boarding house and was well known as a stout patriot who "never concealed her opinions" according to Dr. Andrew Anderson, a witness to subsequent events, as reported in the book *Hours With The Living Men and Women of the Revolution* by oral historian Benson John Lossing.

The British had claimed the right of possession of New York City until noon on Evacuation Day, but Mrs. Day was having none of it.

Soon after breakfast that day, she proudly went outside and displayed the stars and stripes flag for all to see on a nearby pole.

Around 9 a.m. that same morning, Dr. Anderson, lounging idly on the porch outside his home, observed a "burly red faced British officer in full uniform walking rapidly in the direction of the flag."

Mrs. Day was quietly sweeping the street outside her door when the officer came upon her and screamed, "Who hoisted that rebel flag?"

Mrs. Day stopped sweeping and stated: "It is not a rebel flag, sir, but the flag of a free people."

"Pull down that flag," roared the officer.

"Who are you?" Mrs. Day asked.

"I'm His Majesty's provost-marshal, charged not to let a rebel flag fly in this town before noon today. Pull down that flag."

"I will not do it," Mrs. Day replied. "If the king himself stood where you did and commanded me to pull it down I wouldn't do it."

Several cries of approval and huzzahs could be heard from nearby neighbor's homes.

"You cursed rebels in petticoats," exclaimed the officer. "If you were not a woman I'd hang you on the spot. That rebel flag shall come down."

He seized the halyards. Mrs. Day sprang forward and, with her broom, struck the intruder with heavy and rapid blows.

The burly Briton was knocked down. Eventually he stood up and snatched his hat from the ground, muttering curses and slinking off, never to return.

The first free American flag ever flown in New York fluttered quietly in the gentle breeze. The British were gone after more than 160 years of dominance in America.

The world was upside down.

CHAPTER 1

Hercules Mulligan, Thinker, Tailor, Sleeper Spy

On the morning after Evacuation Day, November 25, 1783, George Washington, newly resident in New York, kept a breakfast engagement.

He was the hero of the hour, feted the night before at Fraunces Tavern by Governor Clinton of New York and many other leading figures. He was the magnificent leader of a brand new nation that, even then, looked likely someday to be the most powerful on earth.

He had just held a farewell morning parade in Bowling Green. The British ships had sailed for home after seven years of occupying New York; their grasp on world domination shattered for all time. Their ignominious defeat at the Battle of Yorktown in 1781 dealt a fatal blow to their empire building and willingness to fight.

Even the mad King George III knew the jig was up—the cost of supplying an army in America a crushing burden at a time when the British economy was in dire straits. It was time to wind down. America would be free.

From Yorktown on, the outcome of the fight was inevitable and the capture of New York by the rebels on that famed clear and crisp November day two years later was merely the coda to a magnificent American campaign. The British drummers and fife had allegedly played a tune called "The World Turned Upside Down" after the Yorktown defeat.

Indeed it was. The signing of the Treaty of Paris ended hostilities between the United States and Great Britain on September 3, 1783. But such was the panicked mass seeking to get out that it took until November for the British and many of their loyalist American supporters to evacuate. Suddenly, Washington had become a worldwide legend—the indomitable general who whipped an army of peasants, farmers, militia members, and poor city dwellers into such fighting trim that they had defeated what was considered the most powerful army on earth.

Washington had help from the French, but his leadership was unquestioned.

On Tuesday, November 25, 1783—known as Evacuation Day ever since—with the British ships beyond the horizon, Washington would lead his men in a victory parade on Broadway.

The contrast between the departing British Army—all spit and polish and serried files—and the ragtag army of Washington was so remarkable that a young female onlooker wrote, per the *New York Times*:

> The troops just leaving us were as if equipped for show and with their scarlet uniforms and burnished arms, made a brilliant display. The troops that marched in, on the contrary, were ill clad and weather-beaten, and made a forlorn appearance. But then, they were our troops, and as I looked at them, and thought upon all they had done for us, my heart and eyes were full, and I admired and gloried in them more because they were weather beaten and forlorn.

Each soldier wore a black and white cockade in honor of the French who had played such a role in their victory. They marched eight abreast as the delirious New Yorkers jammed the footpaths along the Bowery to see for themselves this all-conquering General George Washington who had capsized the unbeatable British. Benjamin

Tallmadage, Washington's key intelligence officer, painted the scene in his memoir: "Gen. Knox at the head of a select corps of American troops entered the city soon after which the Commander-in-Chief, accompanied by Gov. Clinton and their respective suites, made their public entry into the city on horseback followed by the Lieut-Governor and members of the Council."

But it was Washington who was the cynosure of all eyes.

He fitted the physical notion of a peerless leader. A contemporary description stated he was "measuring six feet two inches in his stockings and weighing 175 pounds . . . His frame is padded with well-developed muscles, indicating great strength." By all accounts, he was one of the best horsemen in the Continental Army and fearless in battle.

Many people wanted him as their king, and with a nod of his head the kingdom would have been his. But Washington would not betray his Republican ideals and soon after resigned from military life. They wanted him as king again after he served four years as president but Washington again ignored their blandishments, thereby setting in stone the notion of democratic government.

Washington would celebrate at Cape's Tavern with Governor George Clinton and nine days later would make his famous farewell speech to his troops at nearby Fraunces Tavern—still standing today—a speech which has been read out every year since by a member of the US congress on Washington's Birthday, February 22.

Like Cinncinatus, the farmer who became a general, and then returned to his plough after leading the defense of Rome in about 490 BC, Washington was returning to the land in his beloved Virginia after leading the new American army to a great victory.

He said in his famous speech: "With a heart full of love and gratitude, I now take leave of you. I most devoutly wish that your later days may be as prosperous and happy as your former ones have been glorious and honorable."

If things had turned out differently, he made clear where his last stand would have been: "If defeated everywhere else, I will make my stand for liberty, among the Scots-Irish in my native Virginia."

But there was no need for that. Thanks in part to the Scots Irish and Irish Catholics, Washington had carried the day.

Indeed, just a few months later, on April 2, 1784, Lord Mountjoy would go on to lament in the British Parliament that "America was lost by Irish emigrants . . . I am assured from the best authority, the major part of the American Army was composed of Irish and that the Irish language was as commonly spoken in the American ranks as English. I am also informed it was their valor that determined the contest."

It is not known where Mountjoy was taking his facts from, but modern scholarship has certainly shown the Irish role to have been far greater than was supposed.

On November 26, the day after Evacuation Day, Washington would certainly make immediately clear how important the Irish had been to him, especially one man.

On his first triumphant day in charge, when he could have met with any number of his greatest generals, dignitaries, or politicians, or attended a hundred breakfasts in his honor, Washington mounted his horse Nelson, a handsome chestnut. From where he was staying at Number One Broadway, the former residence of Archibald Kennedy, one of the wealthiest men in Manhattan, he rode for a half a mile toward where 219 Pearl Street now stands.

There he was going to break his fast with an obscure Irishman from County Derry, once a plain immigrant, living not in a gilded palace or grand hotel but an unremarkable small townhouse.

In Washington's time, the house's address was 23 Queen Street.

It was Washington's clear intent on this day after the greatest of days to show the world how much he valued the secret role of the man who lived there, one Hercules Mulligan, then aged forty-three years. Mulligan's father Hugh, a deep reader of Greek philosophy and myth, had conferred the strange first name on him—so strange that some believed it was a pseudonym.

Washington must have cut a fine figure: a superb horseman, a great general, the father of the new country. But who was this Hercules Mulligan, this haberdasher he wanted so urgently to meet? The fancy set was at a loss to explain it.

Yet Washington knew that as one of his most valuable spies, Mulligan had made a profound difference in the war.

Washington certainly felt a debt needed to be repaid. As noted in the *Recollections and Private Memoirs of Washington*: "he breakfasted with M-----, to the wonder of the Tories and the perfect horror of the Whigs." Mulligan had saved Washington's life on at least two occasions, historians agree, while putting his own life at risk again and again.

Frederick Hitz, former CIA inspector general, revealed in his book *Why Spy? Espionage in an Age of Uncertainty* that former CIA Director William Casey remarked to him in the 1980s that if he had his way the statue of martyred spy Nathan Hale at the then CIA Headquarters in Langley, Virginia, would be replaced by one of Hercules Mulligan. According to Casey, the Irishman was possibly America's best ever espionage agent.

Washington also knew that it was Mulligan who had sharpened the steel of a young migrant who had stayed in Mulligan's home for an extended period after he'd landed in America.

His name was Alexander Hamilton, and Mulligan is widely credited with turning him from a royalist into a revolutionary. The two spent hours talking when Hamilton was Mulligan's guest, and there is no doubt the Irish rebel had a major impact on the future statesman. The two men became close in life and even in death, as they are buried next to each other in a New York churchyard.

Mulligan was what became known as a "stay behind agent" when the British took New York. He originally sought to flee but was unable to escape and continued his job as a master tailor.

His wife was the niece of a British admiral; his brother worked for a company that supplied necessary goods to the Redcoats; and Mulligan's loyalist credentials and expert skills as a tailor made him a favorite with the British.

Partly because of his strong loyalist links, he did a roaring trade. Newspaper ads at the time featuring Mulligan's store talk of a "Clothing Emporium" with "superfine clothes of the most fashionable colours, gold and silver spangled buttons, gold epaulets for gentlemen of the army."

For years amidst the dandies, the young posers, and the Redcoat generals, Mulligan went doggedly about his task. Years later, he told Benjamin Tallmadge, the chief of intelligence for Washington, his stealthy methods of spying: "Generals have a way of talking sometimes when they are being fitted for an embroidered waistcoat . . . so I keep my ears open."

A few glasses of the finest port also helped, as did the jovial nature of Mulligan who completely put clients of soldiers, officers, and generals at ease.

Unknown to the many Redcoats and dandies who sought the finest clothes and uniforms, Mulligan was part of the Culper spy ring: men and women who risked their lives to carry information from behind enemy lines. (The name Culper referred to a local town in Virginia near where George Washington lived.)

The ring was put together at Washington's insistence. He knew he was outnumbered on the battlefield and his men lacked vital experience, but cracking enemy intelligence would go a long way to leveling the playing field.

Washington knew the importance of a good spy. "There is nothing more necessary than good intelligence to frustrate a designing enemy, and nothing that requires greater pains to obtain," he wrote.

The Culper men and women were clever. They used invisible ink, an incredible invention for the time. They used couriers who never knew each other but left vital messages in tree hollows. A female member of the ring, Anna Strong, displayed her washing on the clothesline in a certain way when she had information. They rowed across Long Island Sound to Connecticut, where Washington was camped, so they would not encounter check points.

They put the name of a British commanding officer on their secret envelopes on the grounds that any soldiers accosting them would be more reluctant to open such letters.

Their influence was enormous, their role dangerous, and their spirits daring.

But of all of them, the man Washington was meeting that morning was an extraordinary secret agent—hiding in plain sight, taking huge risks, and seemingly impossible to track. The British knew someone at a very high level was operating in New York but it would take the traitor Benedict Arnold to unmask him. Even then, the British were not sure.

Indeed, Mulligan had performed so perfectly that right after the war some citizens of the new republic suspected him of being a loyalist and wanted him hanged as a traitor.

The Mulligan accusers were thus in deep shock and denial when Washington showed up at the home and emporium of Hercules with its sign that read "H MULLIGAN CLOTHIER."

After Washington was welcomed and bought a uniform in the shop following their breakfast, Mulligan quickly replaced the sign with "H MULLIGAN CLOTHIER TO GENERAL WASHINGTON." He would continue to supply Washington with uniforms and necessities when Washington was in the White House and beyond.

That November morning, there's no doubt Mulligan knew Washington was coming, and being a spy he also likely knew his eating habits.

He and his slave, Cato, discussed the preparations. At the time, 20 percent of the population of New York was slaves.

Mulligan later despised slavery and was among the leaders of the manumission group in New York to end slavery forever, according to Alexander Hamilton biographer and historian Ron Chernow.

Cato played a key role in conveying intelligence information through Redcoat lines where an ordinary slave would hardly be glanced at. Yet, because he was black, he has effectively been written out of history.

(In a nice touch in the Broadway production of *Hamilton*, Hercules Mulligan is typically played by a black man, and Cato is given full voice at last.)

They would have prepared Washington's favorite breakfast meal which consisted of tea or coffee and cold corn beef, cold mutton, and, of all things, chocolate.

Chocolate for breakfast was all the rage, a fad that may have been started by Washington or, more likely, his wife Martha Custis.

They weren't against converting others to their cause, either, as is evidenced by a letter from Washington's aide-de-camp Burgess Ball. On February 3, 1794, he wrote to Washington requesting he send him "two or three bushels of chocolate shells." He added that he had "frequently drank Chocolate off at Mt. Vernon, as my wife thinks it agreed with her better than any other Breakfast."

Much of the information on the life of Hercules Mulligan comes from a brief 1937 biography of him simply entitled *Hercules Mulligan* and written by one Michael J. O'Brien.

O'Brien is little known but was a formidable historian—a fact recognized in 1932 when the National University of Ireland endowed him with an honorary master's degree for his work on the Irish in the Revolutionary War.

O'Brien wrote massively and extensively on the Irish role and was the official historian of the American Irish Historical Society and the Friendly Sons of Saint Patrick.

His obituary in the *New York Times* of November 13, 1960 characterized O'Brien as having "established the facts about the very large Irish population in the colonies at the time of the Revolution and the important part they played."

According to O'Brien, Mulligan had revealed himself early in life as virulently anti-British. Born in Coleraine, County Derry, he and his family were forced out of Ireland when Hercules was six. They were Presbyterians and dissenters, groups which would go on be key figures in the ill-fated 1798 uprising against the British in Ireland led by Theobald Wolfe Tone and which drew heavily on Northern dissenters.

Hercules Mulligan became an Anglican later in life, perhaps because his wife, who had royal connections, was from that tradition and it helped him with his own career. Nonetheless, he also contributed heavily to the upkeep of a Scottish Presbyterian church.

Dissenters were mostly descended from Scottish Presbyterians who were given land in the plantation of Ulster in 1609 after William of Orange had defeated the Catholic King James I.

But the dissenters were hated both by the established Anglican Church and the Catholics whose land they had taken as a spoil of war.

Presbyterians suffered greatly from discrimination as a result and were also targets of the Penal Laws—a series of draconian laws created to end all opposition to the Anglican Church in Ireland.

Many of the Presbyterians made their way to America where they were greeted with open arms; thus began the Scots Irish diaspora which would eventually provide seven US presidents—most notably Andrew Jackson, who was born very shortly after his family reached American shores.

As for Catholics, Michael J. O'Brien also minutely traced the Irish Catholics who left Ireland at the time and who played an outsized role in the American Revolution.

According to the *Directory of American History*: "Approximately 50,000 to 100,000 Irish (over 75% Catholic) came to the American colonies in the 1600s. During the 18th century, more than 100,000 additional Irish Catholics arrived, many as indentured servants. In the 1740s, nine out of ten indentured servants were of Irish origin."

As for the Scots Irish, the *Directory* says: "An estimated 250,000 Scots Irish migrated to America during the colonial era. Most colonial settlers coming from the Irish province of Ulster came to be known in America as the '*Scotch-Irish*'. They were descendants of Scottish and English tenant farmers who had been settled in Ireland by the British government during the 17th-century Plantation of Ulster."

Irish immigrants of this period participated in significant numbers in the American Revolution. Tough as teak, contrarian, self-reliant, and no lovers of the British king, the Scots Irish were soon in the thick of it, while the Catholic Irish needed little incentive to join the fight against the old enemy. Unlike new arrivals from Britain, there was no complexity to their choice. The curse of Oliver Cromwell's murderous campaign against Catholics in Ireland was deep in their memories. They would fight with whoever was fighting the British.

Washington's adopted son Custis made clear his father's debt to the Irish of both backgrounds in a speech, quoted by both Presidents Reagan and Obama when they first visited Ireland.

George Washington's son said: "When our friendless standards were first unfurled, who were the strangers who first mustered around our staff? And when it reeled in the light, who more brilliantly sustained it than Erin's generous sons?"

One of those generous sons was Hercules Mulligan.

When the Mulligan family left Coleraine to come to America, they were not penniless like many of their compatriots.

A clue to their status lies in the fact that the Mulligan family arrived in America not as "redemptioners"—that is, indentured servants—but as paying passengers, which indicated a certain status even as they came ashore.

Hugh Mulligan, father of Hercules, was listed a freeman of New York City in November 1747, again proving the Mulligans were viewed as successful immigrants.

Hugh is first listed as a wigmaker but later he switched to mercantile work and ran an importing company on the waterfront.

His three sons soon joined him.

Young Hercules was highly educated for the time. He attended the nearest school run by an Irish emigrant: one Master James O'Brien, who educated the children of many city leaders.

From an early age, rebellion coursed through Hercules Mulligan's blood, perhaps encouraged by the Irish school master. In addition, being forced to leave Ireland ensured that the American patriot spirit was infused in him.

Thus, when the Americans began to demand their own country and republic, and to actively work toward overthrowing the crown, Hercules Mulligan was in the New York vanguard.

After a decent education in the context of the times, he found employment as a young man in his father's importing business and later as a tailor. As it happened, his chosen employment as a tailor would make him invaluable to the Revolution.

The times were rapidly changing. The Stamp Act of 1765, which re-imposed British taxation on American colonists, and the Boston Tea Party of 1773, when the colonists' desire to break the ties with Britain reached a fever pitch, meant the distant drums of war came closer every day. Mulligan was soon in the fray.

His fiery republicanism, however, did not stop him marrying Elizabeth Sanders on October 27, 1773. Sanders was the niece of Admiral Charles Sanders, a high ranking officer in the Royal Navy who later became First Lord of the Admiralty. For Mulligan, his esteemed connection would prove invaluable when he came under suspicion.

He joined, perhaps even as a founding member, the Sons of Liberty, the major underground organization aimed at ending British rule.

Along with major demonstrations each year, they celebrated the repeal of the Stamp Act in 1766. Every Saint Patrick's Day, a toast was drunk by the Sons of Liberty to "Prosperity to Ireland's worthy sons and daughters of Saint Patrick."

Mulligan had become an important figure. He was one of the New York patriot leaders who sat in judgement of Gilbert Forbes, one of the leading Tories, who was accused of setting plans to kidnap key patriot leaders.

Mulligan sat on the committee of enquiry and, when Forbes tried to deny and deflect the charges, Mulligan, as quoted in the minutes of the meeting, told him: "We have authentic evidence of you having been concerned in a hellish conspiracy . . . I advise you to conceal nothing as you hope for pardon."

Mulligan was clearly a key leader in the group and was nominated in 1775 for a seat in the newly-created radical colonial government. But perhaps most important of all was the relationship between Mulligan and a callow young man just off the boat from the British West Indies whom Mulligan generously housed after his arrival in New York, giving him a place of honor in his own household.

This young man was none other than Alexander Hamilton.

The Sons of Liberty: Mulligan and Hamilton

It would be hard to nominate a legendary American hero who started life with less expectation than Alexander Hamilton.

He was born on the island of Nevis, then part of the British West Indies. His birth occurred outside of wedlock to Rachel Faucette and wealthy Scotsman James Hamilton, in either 1755 or 1757. His mother died when he was fifteen, leaving Hamilton effectively orphaned, as his father abandoned him.

Though an orphan, Hamilton proved himself a brilliant polemicist and superb writer, as well as a reliable business partner. He longed for a war and a chance to prove himself. He was idealistic and hated the horrific treatment of slaves in the sugar cane fields. He particularly detested the shocking mortality rates—with three out of five field slaves dying within five years, literally worked to death.

After a massive hurricane destroyed the island in 1772, he wrote such a forceful and descriptive account that the business leaders in Nevis decided to pay his passage to the United States where they probably thought he would garner a top class education and return to his childhood home in excellent shape to help transform it. Hamilton, however, had very different ideas.

Hamilton sailed from Nevis with the name of Hercules Mulligan as one of his few contacts in New York. Hugh, the brother of Hercules, worked for a successful trading business between New York and Bermuda and had strongly recommended to the young man he make contact with Hercules.

It was a fortuitous recommendation. Hercules Mulligan wrote extensively later in his life about his relationship with Hamilton and the immediate rapport between them. Hamilton had arrived with letters of introduction to "Certain agreeable and distinguished persons in New York."

Hercules was top of the list and the young man took lodging with him. Gertrude Atherton, author of *The Conqueror: Being the True and Romantic Story of Alexander Hamilton*, wrote that Mulligan was a good-natured Irishman who received Hamilton hospitably and "asked him to stop in his modest house until his plans were made."

Hamilton clearly felt at home. In Mulligan's late life narrative, he recalled that Hamilton, in the long evenings, "would sit with my family and my brother's family and write doggerel verse for their amusement."

Hamilton, he remembered, was "always amiable and cheerful and extremely attentive to his books."

The two men also talked about war. The coming clash with the English crown was a considerable topic of discussion, and the fiery Mulligan did not hold back in his hard-edged belief that the crown must be vanquished.

Historians have speculated that it was Mulligan who stirred independence fervor in Hamilton, despite the fact that he was originally thought to be of royalist sympathies.

If he did hold such sympathies at some point in his life, all doubt was soon dispelled after Hamilton's fiery speech at a patriot rally.

In July 1774, in the Fields, a large common area which is now located near City Hall in New York, Hamilton showed the impact Mulligan had had on him with a clarion call to action. His speech as it was reported in the local media dealt with "British oppression and the duty of resistance." Mulligan must have been delighted with his eighteen-year-old prodigy.

Mulligan led, or was part of, countless protests against British rule, many of which Hamilton attended with him.

But with the British knocking at the gates of New York City in 1776, intent on putting down the insolent American rogues who had dared to rebel against their king, it was clear war was at hand and the well-drilled Redcoats were more than ready for the fray.

Hamilton was also ready. He was already the captain of an artillery company created by New York's provincial congress, and soon he would attract the attention of Washington himself and become one of his chief aides.

There was absolutely no question where Mulligan and Hamilton stood. The new friends had proudly cast their die together.

Mulligan knew he too was a marked man. He was known by the royalist agents in the city who were awaiting the arrival of General Howe and his British battalions.

Hamilton gained further public notice for his actions after a mass rally following the reading of the Declaration of Independence on the New York City Commons, July 9, 1776, amid great fervor and hullabaloo.

George Washington himself had ordered it read and it marked the moment in history where the gauntlet was thrown down by the colonists to the British. Henceforth, there was no going back, though anyone looking at the rag tag peasant army would never have given it a shot against the finest fighting force in the world.

In the aftermath of the Declaration of Independence reading, Mulligan was among those who led the excited crowd along Broadway to Bowling Green where a statue of mad King George III mounted on his horse stood.

Reports say it was Mulligan who lassoed the rope around the horse's neck and, with the help of others, toppled the statue.

The crowd also removed all of the crown ornaments that topped the fence around the statue. They were used to make forty thousand musket balls for the fledgling army of the Republic.

The euphoria was short lived. The British forces advanced on New York at speed, and Washington was immediately faced with the critical decision: did he stand and fight or beat an organized retreat?

Hamilton had studied the battle lines after crossing over to Brooklyn and realized there was looming defeat if Washington stood his ground on Long Island. For an eighteen-year-old to have such a confident strategic analysis was truly uncanny. He sent an urgent, anonymous message to Washington to avoid a Long Island battle and live to fight another day. He also outlined an alternative strategy.

George Washington Parke Custis, grandson of Washington, later wrote about the uncanny military mind that Hamilton possessed and, in addition, revealed it was Mulligan—in the first exercise of his spy craft—who delivered the message to Washington who, alas, never took the advice.

On August 26, General William Howe's men broke through to Manhattan Island at the Battle of Kips Bay and thereafter inflicted one stinging defeat after another on the Americans.

It was clear New York City would fall. Mulligan had good reason to fear what would happen to him as a prominent member of the Sons of Liberty. He bundled his wife and son into a carriage and sought to flee north toward upstate New York, possibly intending to head for Canada.

He was intercepted around where City Hall now stands. Ironically, his arrest came at the command of Sheriff William Cunningham, a native Irishman who paid full fealty to the Crown.

Unfortunately for Mulligan, he had history when it came to Cunningham. About a year earlier, the two men had clashed and Mulligan had dragged him by the neck around the Fields and demanded he abjure the king.

Cunningham refused and the fiery Mulligan stripped him of all his clothes, leaving him naked and covered in mud.

Now, the tables had turned, and Mulligan was the vulnerable one. Mulligan was thrown in jail and his wife and son sent back home.

Luckily for Mulligan, Cunningham sought long and hard but had no direct evidence of Mulligan's membership in the Sons of Liberty, and thus he was forced to let his prisoner go. Mulligan returned home to Queen Street and back to his haberdashery and tailor shop mightily relieved, no doubt, that he had slipped through the fingers of the Redcoats.

As a stay-behind spy, Mulligan was playing a very dangerous game. He was right in the maw of the British, entertaining and fitting out their officers many hours of the day while harvesting every scrap of information they unwittingly relayed.

But he was about to reach unheard-of heights. His close connection to Hamilton would bring Mulligan inside the inner sanctums of Washington's top spies, and lead to him playing an incredible role during the war itself. For it was Hamilton who drew Mulligan into Washington's inner spy circle. Hamilton was seeking Washington's attention. He was a self-taught military strategist who constantly amazed those who drilled with him with his knowledge of the intricacies of war and weaponry. It was only a matter of time before Washington heard about this dashing young commander and asked him to serve as his chief military aide. From orphanhood and exile, barely out of his teen years, Hamilton's achievement of heading Washington's inner circle was truly incredible. His contact with Mulligan, and Washington's insistence on the extensive use of spies, meant Mulligan would become the most trusted spy of all, operating directly in the enemy's lair.

Washington was especially impressed by Hamilton's coolness.

Almost certainly through Hamilton's influence, Mulligan became the key agent in New York City. Confirmation of his importance was the fact that he was named as "Confidential Correspondent of the Commander in Chief" by Washington soon after Hamilton joined the Washington inner circle.

New York was the seat of power for the British, where all the planning for the war was decided and all the intelligence gathering on Washington and other patriot leaders was collated. A spy operating around the invasion forces was invaluable.

The spying was not all one-sided, however. The Redcoats recruited an Irishman, Major John Lynch, to infiltrate the Irish community because the British knew from centuries' old experience that they would be among their most bitter enemies.

Lynch was also tasked with forming an Irish battalion but found few willing Irishmen and could never recruit enough members to do so.

* * *

John Church Hamilton, Alexander's son, himself a fine historian, related an incident of great import that his father had told him about.

General Washington "was appointed to meet some officers at a designated place. Information was given by a female in the tory interest and the necessary arrangements were made to seize him. But timely intelligence frustrated the attempt."

That evidence came when a partisan officer, a native of New York, called at the shop of Mulligan late in the evening seeking a watch coat. The late hour awakened Mulligan's curiosity and, after some enquiries, the officer vainly boasted that before another day had passed, they would have the rebel general in their hands.

Right from the beginning, the British targeted Washington, seeking to literally cut off the head of the revolution by capturing or killing him. Bribes offering great amounts were made public; deserters were sought; and specially trained units were occupied with seeking him out.

Plots to kill or capture Washington were regularly drawn up. At times, only Hercules Mulligan, it seems, stood between the British and a successful effort to eliminate Washington. The general, of course, was seen by the British (with good reason) as the undying symbol of American resistance.

By visiting his house directly after the Evacuation Day departure, Washington was making clear how important the role of Hercules Mulligan had been to him.

Mulligan saved Washington's life on at least two occasions that we know about.

Unusually for a spy, Mulligan let his targets come to him. From his perch in his tailor shop, he watched and waited. Though by that point he had a steady team of tailors, he always took care of the senior Redcoat officers himself, offering them a glass of wine as he worked.

They suspected nothing. After all, he was married into British high society and seemed a grand fellow. Meanwhile Mulligan measured them well.

He regularly left for Long Island to deliver his intelligence to the Culper spies who would then relay it by couriers or boat to Washington. He appeared to be without fear, even foolhardy as he crossed enemy lines. So daring was he that one of the men he reported to, Adrian Woodhull, took to his bed to avoid meeting him directly when he heard Mulligan was on his way, because the Irishman seemed so reckless and unafraid.

It was highly dangerous work. Nathan Hale, a dashing young patriot spy, was apprehended and sentenced to death. He was subsequently executed on September 22, 1776. His dying words were said to be: "I regret I have only one life to live for my country."

Mulligan was well aware that spies were given no quarter and were either hanged or shot.

Still he persisted.

As the war went on, the haberdashery with the spool and thread on the sign over its door became a mine of information.

Apart from officers with loose lips spreading information around that Mulligan happily gathered up, the tailor often received orders for Redcoat uniforms. By the weight of the cloth that was ordered he was able to predict with accuracy whether the battalion was heading north or south.

His brother Hugh, who worked for a major army supplier, was able to tell Hercules what kind of operation the units were heading into.

His most important notes were sewn into the hem of a new shirt or jacket and sent forth via Cato to Alexander Hamilton or to Long Island to the Culper gang.

Along with his membership in the illegal Sons of Liberty, which had been launched by Samuel Adams and included members such as John Hancock and Paul Revere, Mulligan was now at the center of the clandestine army playing a huge role in the war.

Saving Washington Again

In February 1781, another attempt to capture Washington and crush the morale of the revolutionaries took place.

Washington was on a planned trip to Maine via the Connecticut Shoreline. British General George Clinton became aware of Washington's movement and scrambled a body of cavalry numbering three hundred to intercept and capture or kill the US commander in chief.

This time it was Hugh, Mulligan's brother, who spotted the urgent order for provisions for the cavalry unit along with information that Washington himself was the target.

Hercules Mulligan took the message and, despite the fact that the Washington expedition was well underway, succeeded (either by himself or with Cato) to ride like the dickens and intercept Washington. In response, Washington took a different route and his much smaller force barely avoided the British cavalry.

The communication between Mulligan, Hamilton, and Washington was constant. Doctor Samuel Smucker, author of a 2010 biography of Hamilton titled *The Life and Times of Alexander Hamilton*, noted that both Hamilton and Washington corresponded regularly with Mulligan.

There was one other occasion when we know Mulligan had a profound impact on the war.

In July 1780, Mulligan learned that General Henry Clinton was planning a lightning attack on ten thousand French troops billeted in Rhode Island. Mulligan's warning meant that Clinton ended up chasing wild geese, not the nub of the French Army.

Washington certainly understood how invaluable the Mulligan information had been.

He wrote to Lafayette that "Captain Hamilton informed you yesterday of the advice received from New York of an intended embarkation. Am glad this has given you time to prepare."

Mulligan surely felt the incredible pressure of hiding in plain sight, like a pilot fish swimming just under the nose of a Great White Shark. His extraordinary ability to befriend the enemy while simultaneously betraying them was like a high wire trapeze act—sooner or later he might fall.

Fall he did, and he found himself back in the Provost Jail.

Already under suspicion, Mulligan was a marked man in some loyalist circles. He was known as a fiery Irishman and to be a member of the Sons of Liberty. It was also known he had taken part in mass rallies; had aided in the tearing down of the statue of King George III after the reading of the Declaration of Independence; and was a known associate of Alexander Hamilton.

City Provost (Sheriff) Cunningham had no doubt where Mulligan's sympathies lay and he had him arrested on suspicion of spying. Mulligan had attacked Cunningham after he found him spying on a Sons of Liberty meeting. Cunningham also knew from his own spies that Mulligan was a prominent member of the organization.

But Mulligan had wormed his way so deeply into the affections of the British top brass that they found it impossible to believe, he had been spying on them. Many were frankly astonished that Mulligan was under suspicion. He had covered his tracks and fooled his adversaries well. Until, that is, Benedict Arnold showed up.

Outwitting Benedict Arnold
The traitor arrived in New York in September 1780 and took refuge onboard a British warship.

He was immediately given the title of brigadier general and was asked to reveal everything he knew about the American intelligence effort which was proving such an impediment for the Redcoats.

Arnold immediately named Mulligan as the key figure, based on conversations with Washington and Hamilton. Suddenly, a hangman's noose was dangling over Mulligan's head.

Mulligan had been accused twice before, and the officers had laughed it off, but this was much more serious. Fifty others were arrested on Arnold's word that they either were spies, or had aided and abetted them.

Mulligan was brought under guard to the Bridewell prison where there was an area reserved for "desperate criminals." He made one effort at escape but was nabbed and returned to the hellish conditions.

He was arraigned in a court martial, with Arnold the main witness against him. But Arnold was despised by the British officer class and failed to win a conviction.

Incredibly, the British officers failed to believe the evidence before their very eyes, so close were they with Mulligan.

However, the court martial proved the end of Mulligan's secret agent career. Though he was freed, suspicions lingered and business in the shop dropped. Soon, he was forced to close and go work in his brother's company.

He had pulled off his subterfuge so well that some American loyalists were certain he was a royalist and nothing would convince them otherwise.

Nothing, that is, until George Washington showed up on his doorstep the day after Evacuation Day to give him his implicit seal of approval, order a suit of non-military clothes now that his shop was again open, and become a friend for life.

Doubtless, the two had an immense amount to discuss over breakfast on that day long ago when Hercules Mulligan, a humble Irish immigrant, was given the august honor of the presence of the future president in his home as well as a personal acknowledgement and a standing order to supply military and non-military clothing to America's greatest hero.

Mulligan went on to live a happy and long life, and would become embroiled—as ever —in the great constitutional issues of his day. His slave Cato, who had risked his own life many times, fades from history at this point but doubtless was the person Mulligan was keen to free when he became one of the founders of the New York Manumission Society.

The anti-slavery pact he signed read in part: "although freed by the laws of God they are held in slavery in the laws of the state." The statement also expressed "pain and regret [for] the miseries which these unhappy people experience from the practice of exporting them like cattle."

* * *

Hercules Mulligan died at age eighty-four on March 4, 1825.

He is laid to rest at Trinity Church in bustling downtown New York, ten paces behind where the grave of the great Alexander Hamilton lies. In death, as in life, they are close together —two immigrant sons who played a uniquely extraordinary role in the creation of the United States. They led by example and millions followed.

Hamilton: An American Musical

Incredibly, 187 years after Hercules Mulligan passed on, his life and legend became an integral part of the Broadway monster hit *Hamilton*, written and arranged by Lin-Manuel Miranda.

Once again, this time on stage, Hamilton and his mentor and friend Hercules Mulligan take to the New York streets as revolution and renewal of the American dream of freedom once more stalk the boards. It is one of the greatest Broadway hits of all time. In the original Broadway production, actor Okieriete Onaodowan played Mulligan.

Here is a brief summation of his role:

> Hercules Mulligan is a friend and mentor of Alexander Hamilton and lives a dangerous double life as George Washington's key US spy in British-occupied New York.

In Act 1, Hercules Mulligan first appears where he, the Marquis de Lafayette, and John Laurens demand to know Aaron Burr's intentions and seek to discover why he is slowing down the revolution.

Later, he reveals that he is a tailor's apprentice and seeks to fight the British. He joins the chorus of voices singing about a new dawn for America.

Mulligan joins the leaders of the Sons of Liberty, a radical group dedicated to American independence. On the eve of war, Mulligan carouses with his fellow fighters and sings of hope for a new country.

Mulligan signs up for the revolution, and joins his fellow patriots as they prepare for war.

Mulligan, however, will never see a battlefield. He returns to his tailor business and becomes an invaluable spy at Hamilton's request. After some years, and a successful outcome, Mulligan reveals to his comrades he has been a chief spy for General Washington. Mulligan sings of his great joy at achieving freedom but warns Hamilton that the hand of history is on him. Mulligan does not appear in the second act.

Washington's Remarkable Irish Women

From his beloved seventy-two-year-old housekeeper to ragged camp followers to society dames to an adored doctor and "Angel of the Camps," Irish women played a critical role in Washington's Revolution.

CHAPTER 2

Mary Waters, Angel of the Camps

The Philadelphia Directory of 1796 lists Dublin-born immigrant Mary Waters as "widow" and "doctoress." In 1777 she was listed also as "apothecary" or pharmacist and later, in 1798 and 1799, as "doctoress" again.

It was highly unusual for a woman to be listed as the equivalent of a doctor and as a qualified pharmacist too, but Mary Waters defied expectations all her life.

The brief entries belie the fact that Mary Waters—penniless Irish emigrant, nurse, doctor, and apothecarist—is one of the great untold Irish stories of the American Revolution, during which she served as a nurse to Washington's army.

She was so beloved that Washington's surgeon general, Benjamin Rush, began a biography of her that was never completed but which was an indication of her elevated standing.

Given the chasm in social and gender terms between the top army surgeon and a mere nurse, a biography of Waters by Surgeon General Rush would truly have been a remarkable departure from class and gender norms.

She was the American equivalent of Florence Nightingale, the heroic British nurse who transformed nursing and sanitary conditions during the Crimean War. Nightingale was known simply as the "Lady with the Lamp" or the "Angel of Crimea."

Waters became famous in American ranks for the same kindness and ability while dealing with horrific conditions, daily exposing herself to cholera and smallpox and other infectious diseases in the rat-ridden military and field hospitals.

There certainly was discrimination at the time on the basis of gender. After all, female nurses at the time were opposed by many military leaders on the grounds that they would distract their fighting men.

Waters soon vanquished the theory that women could be of little importance in the military and field hospitals. Doctor Rush, signatory to the Declaration of Independence, and the most distinguished doctor in America at the time, witnessed her remarkable nursing skills and felt moved to begin a biography.

Alas, those notes were never turned into a book, or at least no book was ever found, but we do have some of Rush's thoughts for posterity on this extraordinary woman.

Rush himself was a remarkable figure; as well as signing the Declaration of Independence, he was surgeon general to the Continental Army, and was present at the Continental Congress.

Benjamin Rush was a renaissance man, a leader in the enlightenment movement, and was called the father of American psychiatry by some because he was among the first to intuit the importance of the brain and to examine mental illnesses among his patients.

He also fought for equality for women, found slavery reprehensible, and fought for better public health measures such as cleaner streets and personal hygiene. On the negative side, at the start of the war he voiced loudly his opinion that Washington was not up to the onerous task of being commander in chief. But he would quickly excise these words from his diary as the war continued and the tide turned.

Despite a rocky start, he became a personal friend of Washington, but, more importantly, he ceaselessly importuned the commander in chief to do something urgently about the desperate state of the Continental field hospitals given what he had witnessed.

He wrote: "Early in the war I feel for our brave countrymen who suffer under our hands . . . I can no longer constrain the distress I feel." He pointed out that the hospitals had less than half the supplies needed for survival.

He lamented that far too many patients were being clustered together in single rooms, leading to the spread of disease. He pointed out there was an enormous lack of bed clothing and that the person in charge, the director general, never even visited the hospitals, before making judgement on how to contain illness and improve the lives of the helpless souls forced to stay in them.

He voiced his concern: "When I consider the present army under your command as the last great hope I am alarmed and distressed at these facts beyond measure."

Rush's plea had the desired effect and matters improved for a time, but when Rush stepped aside as surgeon general the old regime took over once more.

It was under these conditions that Mary Waters was working. She faced immediate prejudice as a woman. Social historian Linda Grant De Paus noted: "All nurses had to confront the hostility of physicians and the belief that no decent woman would nurse a man outside her immediate family."

After the war began, women followed the army and their husbands and became known as camp followers. Many soldiers resented their presence, but Washington realized the invaluable role they could play in cooking, cleaning, and other tasks in order to keep men on the battlefield.

As mentioned, nursing during the Revolutionary War was a dangerous profession that brought you daily into close proximity with deadly diseases such as smallpox and cholera, but treating wounds inflicted by cannon, shell, and rifle were often the most hideous issues to deal with.

Infections meant that you were far more likely to die in the field hospital than in the battle itself. Such injuries suffered on the battlefield also caused great pain and amputations were widespread. The only pain relief available was literally to "bite a bullet" which is where the expression comes from, while the leg or some other part of a limb was being amputated. Often, the task of the nurses was to hold patients down while the doctors did their gruesome work.

The nurses were especially vulnerable to illness themselves. "While surgeons and surgeon mates performed most of the skilled medical duties, female nurses did mostly custodial work, feeding and bathing patients, emptying chamber pots, cleaning hospital wards, and occasionally cooking," according to Rebecca Beatrice Brooks in an article titled "The Roles of Women in the Revolutionary War" published on the History of Massachusetts blog.

They also "changed linen, swept, disinfected hospitals with vinegar, combed hair, and were demanded to stay sober. Nurses provided many of the essential duties that kept the hospitals and camps running," according to nursing historian and writer Julia Tortorica.

In the heat of battle, with injured soldiers arriving in convoys to military hospitals, there was often bedlam. The extraordinary compassion and fearlessness of Nurse Mary Waters in such dire circumstances won the attention of Doctor Rush.

Rush wrote: "She was born in Dublin [and] possesses a good deal of skill and an uncommon regard to cleanliness . . . great danger rouses her into great activity and humanity. (She) served during the whole war in the military hospitals and was esteemed and beloved by all who knew her. I never saw her out of humor . . . she is chatty and tells a merry story very, very agreeably." Rush continued: "The late Reverend Mr Farmer told her that her skill in nursing was a commission sent to her in heaven which she was bound never to resign and that she might merit heaven by it."

She was "minutely acquainted with the characters, manners habits of all the physicians in town," he added.

Clearly, she was often sent for even before doctors were. She was careful always to give the physicians the credit, but the fact that so many wanted her to treat them spoke volumes. Rush explained she was sought out by many patients who preferred her to deal with their illnesses, such as consumption, for her skills—both medical and pharmaceutical—were known to so many people.

He concluded that she was full of the "grace of human charity and compassion. I once knew her lend money to a patient whom she nursed and to the family in which she lodged."

All that is quite an encomium for an Irish nurse who had a wonderful manner with patients, was humane and kind to everyone, no matter the circumstances, and was deeply admired by those who knew her. She was proud to be part of the American struggle for independence, no doubt having memories of how brutal British occupation had been in Ireland.

She fades from history, though we know she was qualified in pharmacy skills as well as in medicine up to the year 1799. Like many of the selfless female nurses, her role would have been edited out and forgotten were it not for Benjamin Rush writing so profoundly about her. Washington's heroes, Rush was saying, were not only on the battlefield.

Waters was just one of many females who pitched in. Martha Washington and Abigail Adams were also among them. One witness quoted in the *Journal of the American Revolution* stated: "I never in my life knew a woman so busy from the early morning until late at night as was Lady Washington, providing comforts for the sick soldiers." Adds Julia Tortorice: "Abigail [Adams] also served as a nurse and supply deliverer, as well as an ammunition producer."

That these visible women were working for the first time outside the family home turned into something of a door opener for women of following generations to seek work outside the home.

"Some historians believe that women's participation in the American Revolution contributed to the emerging role of Republican Motherhood which assigned women the responsibility for the moral training of their sons for citizenship and which led to the expansion of educational opportunities for women," says a non-bylined article on the "History of American Women." We don't know when exactly Mary Waters came to America, or whether she married, or details of her family life, but we do know she became a heroic figure to many at the time and enhanced women's freedoms by showing how carefully and compassionately women like her could minister to the victims of war. The Revolutionary War was a pivotal point in re-orientating the role of men and women, particularly in the Army and the workforce. Mary Waters played an important role in showing how women were equal with men in terms of ability and caring.

CHAPTER 3

The President's Beloved Housekeeper and Washington's Kindness

Elizabeth Thompson is one of the most intriguing Irish characters who traveled alongside George Washington during and after the Revolutionary War.

She was the elderly head of his household and oversaw about two dozen staff for five years during the war, constantly moving with the commander in chief as he frequently changed residences to keep the British off his trail.

Little is known about her personally. Thompson was her married name and it seems very likely she was of the Presbyterian faith, a fact learned through her will, through which she left her possessions to a Presbyterian church in New York.

Incredibly, she was seventy-two when she took the job in July 1776. It was a post which involved a very heavy workload, not least attending to the general's comfort when he moved camp, as he did incessantly. By the end of the war, Washington had moved ninety times.

Washington probably saw more of her than anyone other than close family. The two got along famously.

It is hard not to speculate that the warm, down-to-earth Thompson was some kind of replacement for Washington for the flinty mother who had raised him but who, by all accounts, shunned him and failed to recognize his achievements.

Thompson was hired after Mary Smith, her predecessor as housekeeper, was revealed to be a British spy by an anonymous letter. Smith subsequently fled to England. She was thought to be part of the Governor William Tryon plot, the loyalist leader who sought to have Washington killed.

Washington was quite distraught at that discovery and immediately sought a replacement. He wrote to General Clinton in New York for help:

> New York, 28th June, 1776.
> Sir,
>
> Having occasion to part with my Housekeeper, a Mrs Thompson somewhere in your Neighbourhood, is recommended to me as a fit person to supply her place. I therefore give you the trouble of forwarding the Inclosed Letter to her, & beg of you to hasten her to this place or an answer, as I am entirely destitute, & put to much inconvenience for want of discharge the duties of this Office.
>
> I am Sir Your Most Obt Servt

Though then aged seventy-two, Thompson came immediately. Soon she was in charge of all kitchen staff and ensuring the general's comfort and tastes were met in all of his residences. In 1777 alone, he slept in twenty-four different houses.

As historian Nancy K. Loane wrote in the *Journal of the American Revolution*: "Elizabeth Thompson was a key figure overseeing the mobile military household." For five years Thompson traipsed up and down the East Coast preparing scores of different locations for the often-exhausted commander of the Continental Army.

At times of such great stress, one can only imagine how important it was for Washington to see Thompson's familiar face in every different halting place.

It is clear from the tone of their letters in later years that a genuine fondness existed. Washington even took the unprecedented step after the war of offering Thompson a home at Mount Vernon to live out the remainder of her days. However, Thompson, then in her eighties, had too many infirmities to travel.

Her job bore huge responsibilities. Loane explains that: "To help make these transitions go smoothly, the general traveled with a 'military family' that included his aides-de-camp and personal servants as well as two cooks, a laundress, and a housekeeper. Mrs. Elizabeth Thompson, a personable Irish woman, took on the position of Washington's housekeeper for most of the American Revolution."

It was certainly an onerous position, especially for a woman so advanced in age. There were a total of twenty-five employees, led by Isaac the cook, and her job was to ensure dinner was served at 3 p.m. each day as Washington avoided eating late. Then there were the laundresses, the housework, ensuring cutlery was cleaned, and the job of making sure every guest room was ready for its occupant. Thompson always slept in the same house as Washington in order to be available at any time.

Most importantly, Elizabeth was in charge of packing up camp at a moment's notice and moving to the next secret location. One can only imagine the strength of character needed for such constant change. She was also available to answer any domestic questions from Martha Washington.

What was George Washington like in person? Hannah Till, a freed slave who worked alongside Elizabeth Thompson as a cook, was interviewed about him in 1824. She was then 102 years old. Historian John F. Watson said she had good memories of her employer: "She said he was very positive in requiring compliance with his orders; but was a moderate and indulgent master. He was sometimes familiar among his equals and guests, and would indulge a moderate laugh. He always had his lady with him in the winter campaigns, and on such occasions, was pleased when freed from mixed company and to be alone in his family."

Another look at the private George Washington came from Army wife Martha Bland who knew General and Mrs. Washington well, as her husband, Colonel Theodorick Bland, was a friend of the commander in chief. She often went on horseback rides with Washington and wife Martha.

Mrs. Bland found that the commander displayed an "ability, politeness, and attention" that she found charming, saying that occasionally, Washington "throws off the hero, and takes on the chatty, agreeable companion—he can be downright impudent sometimes."

This was the private man who would capsize the world. Elizabeth Thompson would know him as well as anyone bar his family.

We know little about where Elizabeth Thompson hailed from, other than the fact that she was Irish.

She was clearly well liked. Dr. James Thacher, a surgeon for the Continental Army, stated that Mrs. Thompson was "a very worthy Irish woman." Martha Washington, a strict mistress, liked Thompson so much she sought to hire her for Mount Vernon after the war. At that stage, Thompson was seventy-seven, a great age for the time, but obviously holding her years well.

Thompson had been briefly let go by Washington soon after arriving in the army camp because the army was moving to winter quarters. This was before she had struck up a close connection with the commander, but Washington quickly learned to his chagrin that Martha, his wife, very much wanted her back.

On May 1, 1777, General Washington wrote to an aide: "Mrs Washington wishes I had mentioned my intentions of parting with the old Woman before her, she is much in want of a Housekeeper." Elizabeth was soon back permanently.

She was illiterate, so we never get to hear her own voice, but we do have her letters to Washington as dictated by her. The demanding job of housekeeper for General Washington is clear, as well as the affection she felt for him.

The following letter is dated October 10, 1783, and Elizabeth is responding to a request from Washington to lay out the wages and remuneration she had gotten:

> When I had the favour of seeing your Excellency at Princeton you desired that I should make an Account for my Services in your Family to be laid before the Financier.
>
> I came into Your Excellency's Service as Housekeeper in the month of June 1776 with a Zealous Heart to do the best in my Power. Although my Abilities had not the Strength of my Inclinations Your goodness was pleased to approve and bear with me until December 1781 when Age made it necessary for me to retire.
>
> Your Bounty and goodness in that time bestowed upon me the sum of £179.6.8 which makes it impossible for me to render an Account: my Service was never equal to what your Benevolence has thus rated them.
>
> And being now in my Eightieth Year should I ever want, which I hope will not be the Case, I will look up to Your Excellency for Assistance where I am sure I will not be disappointed.
>
> And that the Father of Mercies may pour on you his Choicest Blessings shall ever be the Prayer of
>
> Your Excellency's
Old Devoted Servant
Elizabeth Thompson

Washington acted promptly, not only helping to acquire a war pension for Elizabeth but, as she wrote to Congress, "the General who was always kind to me, and whose countenance was a comfort to me when our affairs were at the worst" had invited her to spend her final days "in his own house"—Mount Vernon. But at eighty-one, Mrs. Thompson had a "heap of infirmities" that made travel impossible

She died in 1788 in New York. Her will bequeathed her silver teapot and cream pot with six teaspoons and tea tongues to help fund a new school for poor Presbyterian children, many of them black, in New York. The school opened in 1789. Her role running George Washington's household placed her in the center of the beating heart of the American Revolution. It was an extraordinary place to be for a former Irish immigrant, and she gained true friendship with Washington and his wife in a way that few could.

Years later, Washington was still asking about her in his letters to friends in New York. It is clear she impacted him greatly and offered safe refuge and rest nightly from the storms of the Revolution.

CHAPTER 4

The Socialites Plan Their Ball as the Irish Camp Followers Almost Starve

Caty Littlefield Greene was a sight to behold; by common consent the most beautiful lady in the top echelon of Washington's army wives, married to one of his most trusted generals, Nathanael Greene.

But she was much more than just an army wife.

Twelve years younger than her husband, who was often away as a consequence of his job as quartermaster, she commanded the social scene and had officers come running to attend to her with the crook of a finger.

Every man in the officer's camp admired her, and every woman wanted to be like her—charming and coquettish as was the fashion of the times and a constant source of gossip and envy.

Her fellow socialite, Lucy Knox, was hardly a similar beauty. She was said to be enormously rotund and prone to garish garb and outlandish hairstyles, but she was undoubtedly the social grand dame of the new American republic taking shape.

Lucy was married to Henry Knox, son of Irish immigrants from Derry, who had become a favorite of George Washington and a legendary general in his army.

The two women ruled the roost in terms of polite American society amid the viciousness of the Revolutionary War, and ensured a lively and vivacious social scene. They prospered in the officers' quarters despite the serious battles at hand.

Their lives couldn't have been more different than those four hundred or so camp follower women living in deplorable conditions on the edge of camp, many speaking in Irish brogues, according to historian Nancy Sloane.

Their fate was to be very different from that of the high society madams, despised and mistrusted as they were by the deeply class-conscious gentry who ran the army and its affairs. When the army disbanded camp, the camp followers were last to leave with the baggage, often forced to walk dozens of miles to the next location.

The toughest moments occurred for the followers in winter camp. Late December 1777 was especially trying. Fourteen thousand weary soldiers in Washington's army reached their winter quarters at Valley Forge on December 19.

The army had marched eight miles from Gulph Mills, and its members were starving, cold, and weary. Their horses were described as "very poor and weak" but there was neither fodder for the horses nor food for the soldiers, save what they could scavenge from raw cornfields on the trek. For the camp women, there were only the fruits of begging or watery soup made from old bones

It was a desperate time even to get to the camp to eat. The long line snaked toward the camp—officers on horseback and soldiers marching. After the soldiers came the baggage wagon and behind them the most miserable sight of all, four hundred women, black and white, suffering equally in their misery. Many were shoeless, dressed in thin and tattered rags, some stumbling from cold and hunger, some carrying children, all walking heads down into the wicked wind.

One woman, likely hitching a ride on a wagon, had slipped off and been crushed by the wagon wheels; the others had no option but to keep going.

It was recorded thus: "One wagon overset and killed one woman." No name, no expression of condolence, just the sad facts.

If there was a more pitiable bunch than the women camp followers in Washington's Army, then it would have been very hard to trace them.

They were shunned and sneered at by all ranks.

Joseph Plumb Martin, a private in Washington's army, wrote an autobiography published in 1830, in which he compared the women to "wild beasts" with a bodily appearance that was "odd and disgusting." Martin especially noted the camp women spoke many dialects, "Irish brogue" among the most prominent.

Chances are, many were indentured servants and probably included large numbers of Northern Irish women.

Of course, we will never know. Illiterate camp women at the very base of the totem pole never got to write their stories. Some were washer women, charged with washing the soldiers uniforms; some were prostitutes and some were cooks; others cleaners. Others were accompanying their husbands the only way they knew how; some had been left homeless and followed the army in order to acquire enough to eat and feed their children.

It was not unheard of that after battles, some of these desperate camp followers would strip the injured and dead of their clothes and possessions. Living through the war involved dreadful decisions.

Some women fought. One name recorded in the annals of history is that of Mary Hays from New Jersey, who famously helped an artillery crew load the cannons after her husband was injured during the Battle of Monmouth. It seems she became the model for Molly Pitcher, a famed heroine of the war who seems likely to be a composite of several women who fought alongside their menfolk.

Some of the Irish names of the camp women have not been entirely lost to history, including Sherlock, Murphy, and Brady, so there is no doubt many were from Ireland. Washington had a deeply priggish attitude to them, too, warning that he wanted the women out of sight at any public event such as marching through Philadelphia. Yet he never banished them, knowing their cooking, cleaning, and washing were essential for camp harmony.

One of the most telling descriptions was of camp followers on the British side who were captured after the Battle of Saratoga.

American diarist Hannah Winthrop noted the women appeared to be "beasts of burden."

She added: "[They] Had a bushel basket on their back to which they were bent double, the women in bare feet clothed in dirty rags such effluvia filled the air."

Most of the women eked out an existence as washerwomen, taking on the tough work of cleaning the uniforms, which were usually covered in muck and mire and sometimes blood.

Such a life was very far from Caty Greene's lived experience.

She was twenty-four years old when she showed up at Valley Forge, no doubt skirting the camp followers to be with the general, on January 6, 1778. She was years younger than her husband, and looked it, with her "gloss black hair and clear cut complexion . . . exquisitely molded hands and feet."

Nathanael Greene doted on his wife and called her "angel." When she arrived at Valley Forge to stay with him, she was immediately the cynosure of all eyes.

As quartermaster of the army, Greene was necessarily away for much of the time while his wife stayed near camp. Home for Greene and her husband, needless to say, did not involve fourteen humans crammed into a small makeshift cabin and condemned to the rock hard ground of a freezing Pennsylvania winter.

The Greenes' home was a fine mansion not far away. It was known as Moore Hall and had been requisitioned from a local Loyalist fat cat.

While in camp, Caty had her portrait painted and accepted gifts and favors and chatted up handsome young officers. She was particularly partial, as a French speaker, to the handsome French men who were on hand to discuss strategy with Washington and his generals.

But, most of all, she planned the grand event of the social season: the Alliance Ball, celebrating the alliance with the French that had been consolidated after the game-changing victory at the Battle of Saratoga. This win convinced King Louis XIV that the Americans could fight and perhaps even be eventually victorious.

During the preparations for the ball, at least in the officers' quarters at the camp, proceedings "took on a festive air" according to historian Nancy K. Loane, author of *Following the Drum: Women at the Valley Forge Encampment*.

Caty moved between Continental Army camps and settled for a time at Middlebrook, New Jersey where, once again, she played hostess and led the social scene. The Greenes held two balls. At one of them, Washington famously danced with Caty for three hours straight. It's likely that tongues began to wag.

Washington did not lack female admirers, as this overwrought letter by a young lady makes very clear:

> We were not long seated when General Washington entered, and bowed to the ladies as he passed round the room. "He comes, he comes, the hero comes!" I involuntarily but softly exclaimed. When he bowed to me, I could scarcely resist the impulse of my heart that almost burst through my bosom, to meet him.
>
> —Miss Charlotte Chambers to her mother,
> Mrs. James Chambers,
> Wednesday, February 25, 1795

Not surprisingly there were rumors and innuendo all his life, most notably a British forgery alleging Washington kept a mistress: an Irish woman from New Jersey named Mary Gibbons. According to the tabloid British press, the source of the "story" was said to be Irish-born traitor Thomas Hickey. He was a former Life Guard [equivalent of a member of the Secret Service] who knew about the trysts and who later planned to assassinate Washington and was executed as a result. The story turned out to be another lurid piece of British fiction aimed at undercutting Washington.

Despite the frigid winter, the dreadful lack of food and clothing, and the continued hardship, Caty and hundreds of other officers' wives maintained hectic social schedules, especially after some French officers arrived in camp. It was all *tres charmant*.

A glimpse into the social calendar revealed two very stark worlds living side by side.

Nowhere was that more obvious than in the contrast between the incredible hardship the female camp followers, many of them Irish, endured in comparison to the gentry. The camp women were in a desperate battle for survival; the society ladies were planning their next ball. Never the twain could meet.

In the end, the role of the Irish washerwomen and camp followers was just as vital in its own way as the distraction and relaxation from battle that the society balls provided.

CHAPTER 5

The Heroic Days and Party Nights of General Henry Knox and Wife Lucy

In her book *Following the Drum: Women at the Valley Forge Encampment*, Nancy K. Loane, an expert on women during the American Revolution, focuses particularly on the grand balls held to celebrate the French Alliance. Four hundred officers and about seventy women attended the ball on February 23, 1779.

The hosts were General Henry Knox, son of Irish immigrants from Derry, Northern Ireland, and his wife Lucy. Knox had become a George Washington favorite after leading the herculean effort to bring sixty tons of cannons three hundred miles from upstate New York, amid treacherous winter conditions, to use against the British at the Siege of Boston in 1775.

Historian Victor Brooks called it "one of the most stupendous feats of logistics" of the entire war. When Knox arrived and the cannons completely exposed the British position, General William Howe sought a parlay and surrendered. After eleven months, Knox had won the siege practically overnight. He would eventually end up as President Washington's secretary of war.

Along the way, Knox distinguished himself at the battles of Brandywine, Trenton, Germantown, and Monmouth. He laid the groundwork for the establishment of West Point, and he led the artillery bombardment at the critical Battle of Yorktown.

He was known as many things—a magnificent soldier; a man who never owned slaves; a compassionate soul who tried to treat Native Americans fairly when he became secretary of war; and a reveler, who played an active part in Washington's army's social whirl.

His background was not that of a notable man. Knox had grown up in dire circumstances in Boston, his father having deserted the family soon after they arrived on the new shore from Derry, Ireland. He was a likable lad, however, and several family friends ensured he got an excellent education at Boston Latin School, where he also became fascinated with books and was very well read.

After Boston Latin he opened a bookstore. It was quite the innovative move back then, and became a popular gathering spot for local intellectuals, British officers, and young ladies seeking to advance their education. One young woman, Lucy Flucker, fell madly in love with him as he did with her. The problem was that her father served as the British secretary of the province of Massachusetts, essentially the governor. Henry Knox, having witnessed the Boston massacre, was outspoken in his anti-British views, no doubt also enhanced by his Irish background.

They married, despite the profound anger of her parents, who couldn't accept that she was marrying a mere bookshop owner, and a possible rebel besides. As the war heated up, her family left for England and she never saw them again.

Lucy was a major socialite known for her powerful sway in society, which led to many negative comments about her. Her rotundity and iconic hair fashions—which usually consisted of her hair swept up in pyramid like fashion held upright by pins and brooches—was especially remarked upon.

"She is fatter than ever which is a great mortification to her," General Nathanael Greene wrote to his no-doubt thin wife. "The general [Knox] is equally fat so one cannot laugh at the other."

The husband and wife were said to weigh 290 pounds and 260 pounds, with General Knox the heavier of the two.

Even Washington enjoyed a joke at Knox's expense. When Washington was crossing the Delaware on Christmas night 1776,

Knox was seated in the boat before him. It is reliably reported that Washington poked Knox with his boot and said "shift that fat ass Harry . . . but slowly, or you'll swamp the damned boat."

The laughter of the enlisted men rang up and down the boats as Washington's quip was repeated. We have no record of what Knox thought. He was certainly fat, but also fearless, and became an indispensable ally to Washington during the war.

His personal life was tragic; only three of his thirteen children lived to adulthood, a drastic tally even by the standards of the times.

Still, he and Lucy loved to gallivant and entertain, though she quickly drew criticism from society rivals. Lucy's dress sense was also questioned. Her attire was "ridiculous," wrote the Marquis de Chastellux. Nabby Adams, daughter of John (who became America's second president) and Abigail Adams stated: "I am frightened when I look at her."

Nonetheless, the Knoxes were in love. Greene noted the couple "appear to be extravagantly fond of each other and I think are perfectly happy." The hero general and the grand socialite certainly knew how to entertain. The annual Alliance Ball, celebrating the decision by the French to enter the war in 1778, was an example.

They threw a marvelous party. The food was sumptuous; the frivolity was marvelous. Thirteen cannon fusillades greeted guests, and there was a fireworks display.

The fireworks lit up the skies as guests were led to a ballroom where Washington himself danced with several ladies, making sure to reserve a special dance for Mrs. Knox, who was light on her feet despite her weight. Supper was around ten, followed by more dancing. Typically, the last guests left around 5 a.m., many firmly in their cups.

As one observer, Doctor James Thacher, wrote: "The anniversary of our alliance with France was celebrated in proper style a few days since near head-quarters, at Pluckemin . . . In the evening a very beautiful set of fire-works was exhibited, and the celebration was concluded by a splendid ball, opened by his Excellency General Washington, having for his partner the lady of General Knox."

It was quite the ball. "The power of description is too languid to do justice to the whole of this great entertainment," the *New Jersey Journal* remarked.

The Knoxes first outdid themselves on July 4, 1775, when five hundred guests attended a banquet at their home. Stragglers were observed at midday the next day, and the Knoxes reported many valuable utensils vanished.

Concerning the couple, writer Nathaniel Hawthorne, who stayed in their mansion, noted that Lucy was a "woman of violent passions and so proud an aristocrat that she would never enter any house in the town that was not her own."

He added: "The general was personally very popular but his wife ruled him."

Following his service, General Knox and his wife sought peaceful country and found it in a beautiful old building in Maine which they restored to glory and called Montpelier. Knox had always admired the ability of Washington and Jefferson to become gentleman farmers after the war and their work to replenish the very earth of their new republic country estates. Fortunately for him, Lucy had inherited a vast tract of land in the District of Maine through her parents. The marriage of Lucy and Henry Knox lasted thirty-six years until 1806 when Henry, in an unfortunate incident, swallowed a chicken bone that lodged in his throat. He was buried at Montpelier with full military honors.

The Duke of Rochefoucauld stated Henry Knox was "one of the worthiest men I have ever known."

Lucy Knox's days of happiness and social power were over. She spent her final eighteen years after her husband's death in near poverty, outliving her fortune and dying broke in 1824.

Life was also unkind to Caty Greene, she of the startling beauty and wife of General Nathanael Greene. She lost her beloved Nathanael to sunstroke on their plantation in Mulberry Grove on the Savannah River in Georgia. After his death, she was left awash in debt.

She married again to Phineas Miller, a businessman, but he died of blood poisoning.

She herself passed away on September 2, 1814, at age sixty-one; her glory days long gone.

Both women in their dotage often dreamed they were back in their glory days, welcoming the cream of American society once more to their great balls that had lit up so many lives during such a difficult time.

They Rode with Washington and Changed the War

Two young Irish officers, chief aides to Washington, made history in their own way. A third young gun fired the shot that changed the course of the war. One gave an extraordinary account of crossing the Delaware, and another invented the name "United States of America."

CHAPTER 6

Eyewitness to History—John Fitzgerald Crossed the Delaware by Washington's Side

The diary entries of Irish-born Colonel John Fitzgerald on Washington's crossing of the Delaware, December 25–26, 1776, are among the most fascinating documents of the War of Independence.

Fitzgerald, a native of Wicklow, came to America in 1769 as a young man, probably born around 1750. He was Roman Catholic and a successful businessman who lived close to Mount Vernon. He was a dear friend of Washington—before, during, and after the Revolutionary War.

He was close to the Jesuits, which might indicate that, like many other Catholics of means in Ireland, he fled to France for education because of the crushing Penal Laws aimed at dismembering Catholicism.

Much of the account of the life of John Fitzgerald and his critical role in guarding Washington and being among his closest allies was first set forth in Martin Griffin's Catholic scholarly journal, *The American Catholic Historical Researches*.

Much of Griffin's material was, in turn, collected in a book called *The American Revolution in the Delaware Valley* by Edward S. Gifford Jr.

Griffin began editing in 1886 and started publishing deeply researched information on the key Catholics around Washington at the time, most notably Fitzgerald, whose diary he accessed. He also researched Stephen Moylan, who served for a time as chief aide to Washington. Moylan would become better known only in recent times when it was proven that he was first to use the name "United States of America" for the embryonic country.

After his spell as chief aide, he formed the legendary Moylan's Dragoons, the best cavalry outfit in the US Army—so famous that one of the most notable songs of that era featured his dragoons.

Fitzgerald's account of the Delaware crossing is one of the very few eyewitness accounts of a landmark moment in American history. The subsequent attack and victory over Hessian mercenaries, who were paid by the British to hold Trenton, was the turning of the tide, as Washington was reeling from several defeats and being chased out of New York.

So bad was the situation that Lord Cornwallis went back to London to inform King George III that the rebellion was all but defeated. Meanwhile, his main general, General William Howe, was setting the party scene alight in New York, resplendent in his Redcoat regalia at numerous events. As far as Cornwallis and Howe were concerned, the war was shut down until spring.

It was a depressing moment for the Patriots, enlightened only by the lines written by English revolutionary Thomas Paine, which Washington had distributed to every man:

These are the times that try men's souls; the summer soldier and the sunshine patriot will, in this crisis, shrink from the service of his country; but he that stands it *now*, deserves the love and thanks of man and woman. Tyranny, like hell, is not easily conquered; yet we have this consolation with us, that the harder the conflict, the more glorious the triumph.

So crossing the Delaware and carrying out a surprise attack in the dead of winter seemed like Washington's only hope. As he readied his men, he told them to stay close to their officers; as usual he exuded calm and control. Fitzgerald's excerpt begins:

Christmas, 6 P.M . . . It is fearfully cold and raw and a snow-storm is setting in. The wind is northeast and beats in the faces of the men. It will be a terrible night for the soldiers who have no shoes. Some of them have tied old rags around their feet, but I have not heard a man complain . . . I have never seen Washington so determined as he is now . . . He stands on the bank of the stream, wrapped in his cloak, superintending the landing of his troops. He is calm and collected, but very determined. The storm is changing to sleet and cuts like a knife . . .

[3 A.M.] I am writing in the ferry house. The troops are all over, and the boats have gone back for the artillery. We are three hours behind the set time . . . [the fishermen directing the boats] have had a hard time to force the boats through the floating ice with the snow drifting in their faces. . .

It was broad daylight when we came to a house where a man was chopping wood. He was very much surprised when he saw us. "Can you tell me where the Hessian picket is?" Washington asked. The man hesitated, but I said, "You need not be frightened, it is General Washington who asks the question." His face brightened, and he pointed toward the house of Mr. Howell.

It was just eight o'clock. Looking down the road I saw a Hessian running out from the house. He yelled in Dutch and swung his arms. Three or four others came out with their guns. Two of them fired at us, but the bullets whistled over our heads. Some of General Stephen's men rushed forward and captured two. The others took to their heels, running toward Mr. Calhoun's house, where the picket guard was stationed, about twenty men under Captain Altenbockum. They came running out of the house. The captain flourished his sword and tried to form his men. Some of them fired at us, others ran toward the village.

The next moment we heard drums beat and a bugle sound, and then from the west came the boom of cannon. General Washington's face lighted up instantly, for he knew that it was one of [General John] Sullivan's guns.

We could see a great commotion down toward the meeting house, men running here and there, officers swinging their swords, artillerymen harnessing their horses. Captain Forrest unlimbered his guns. Washington gave the order to advance, and rushed on to the junction of King and Queen streets. Forrest wheeled six of his cannons into position to sweep the streets. The riflemen under Colonel Hand and Scott's and Lawson's battalions went upon the run through the fields on the left to gain possession of the Princeton Road. The Hessians were just ready to open fire with two of their cannons when Captain [William] Washington and Lieutenant [James] Monroe with their men rushed forward and captured them.

We saw [Colonel Johann] Rall [commander of the Hessians] riding up the street from his headquarters, which were at Stacy Potts' house. We could hear him shouting in Dutch, "My brave soldiers, advance."

His men were frightened and confused, for our men were firing upon them from fences and houses and they were falling fast. Instead of advancing they ran into an apple orchard. The officers tried to rally them, but our men kept advancing and picking off the officers. It was not long before Rall tumbled from his horse and his soldiers threw down their guns and gave themselves up as prisoners . . .

[9 P.M.] . . . I have just been with General Washington and [Nathanael] Greene to see Rall. He will not live through the night. He asked that his men might be kindly treated. Washington promised that he would see they were well cared for.

A long account of Fitzgerald is given in Griffin's *The American Catholic Historical Researches* for January 1909 of "Colonel John Fitzgerald, Aide-de-Camp and Secretary to Washington."

Griffin wrote:

> It will be interesting to our readers to gain from this article an idea of the very intimate relations that existed between General Washington and some of the prominent Irish Catholics of his day. One of the first was John Fitzgerald, a young Irishman who settled in that town [Alexandria, Virginia] in 1769 or 1770.
>
> In youthful manhood, he had the reputation of being one of the rising business men and a favorite, even in the social life of the town. It shows social import and intelligence to have, so early, made the acquaintance of Colonel George Washington of Mount Vernon, who, after his services in the French and Indian war, and his cooperation with others against the Stamp Act and other unjustifiable actions of the British ministry, had settled down to the peaceful life of a Virginia planter.

Griffin says that, in December 1770:

> Fitzgerald was elected by Burgess [a councilman] and that, thereupon, he gave a ball at which it is said he first met Mr Washington, though no intimacy resulted from the first interview. The genial young Irishman became readily a favorite with the Scotch and English maidens in Alexandria; but not from them did he choose his wife . . . Fitzgerald, by marrying into a family whose home was opposite to Washington's home, would naturally become on visiting terms with the Washington household, in any event. (Visits by Fitzgerald to Washington's home are recorded on 80 different occasions during this time.) When it came time for war, there was no doubt who Washington wanted by his side.

Griffin wrote: "When Washington, in 1775, in Cambridge, Massachusetts, took command of the Continental Army, under the Old Elm still standing near Harvard Square, Fitzgerald was at his side . . . When the Revolutionary War came on, young Fitzgerald joined the forces of Washington at Cambridge, Massachusetts, as Aide-de-Camp to the General."

Griffin additionally notes that: "In November, the same year, Fitzgerald was appointed one of the secretaries of Washington; as his fellow-Catholic, Stephen Moylan of Philadelphia, had, on March 6, 1776, been appointed secretary to the General, who thus, in the memorable year of Independence, had two Catholics, born in Ireland, as his Aides and Secretaries."

Adds Griffin:

Their worthiness may be judged by Washington's letter to Congress on April 23, 1776, in which he stated: "Aides-de-Camp are persons in whom entire confidence must be placed: it requires men of abilities to execute the duties with propriety and despatch, where there is a multiplicity of business as must attend the Commander-in-Chief of such an army as this; and persuaded I am that nothing [motivates these men] but the zeal of those gentlemen who live with me and act in this capacity, for the great American cause and personal attachment to me."

Fitzgerald and Moylan were not doing it for the money. The pay was thirty-three dollars a month. It was raised to forty dollars. The rank was lieutenant-colonel.

"In all the operations of the army," says Griffin, "Colonel Fitzgerald from 1776 to 1782, save occasional leaves of absence, and then for military purposes, is found constantly by the side of Washington, especially in action. Nor does he appear among those who with 'promptness seek preferment' because of hard duty and inadequate pay; but ever one constant and faithful in devotion to his adopted country and with fidelity and affection for the Commander-in-Chief."

Griffin then alludes to the Conroy plot to replace Washington as commander. Thomas Conroy was himself Irish, from Kerry, and the plotters became known as the Conway Cabal.

As Griffin notes: "At times during the war, intrigues were carried on looking toward the superseding of General Washington by General Gates. Among others concerned was General Conway, who, it was alleged, had written a letter to Gates, containing these or similar words: 'Heaven has determined to save your country, or a weak General and bad councillors would have ruined it.'" Washington turned to Fitzgerald and wrote to him to uncover and expose the plot.

Per Griffin, Fitzgerald replied as follows:

"Alexandria, March 17, 1778. Sir— I am honored with your kind favor of the 28 ult., which I received by last Sunday's post. It gives me the most pleasing satisfaction to find that those who were endeavoring to injure you in the Public esteem, are becoming sensible of their own insignificance & earnestly hope they may feel the contempt and scorn of all good men in proportion to the Iniquitous scheme which they expected to accomplish. Whatever expectations some Individuals in Congress might have formed from joining with this junto . . . " The letter was endorsed in Washington's hand. "Colonel Fitzgerald 17th March 1778."

Under this in a recent hand is written: "Was among General Washington's aides-de-camp of '76. He was a warm-hearted brave and honest Irishman, a merchant of Alexandria before the War."

The plot was foiled in large part by Fitzgerald, once he ascertained who the miscreants were and called them out. As Griffith notes: "It is to the imperishable honor of Colonel Fitzgerald, that, amid Washington's distresses at Valley Forge, he was resolute in upholding the character and fame of the illustrious General . . . Let us honor John Fitzgerald that he was an instrument in unearthing the conspiracy against the 'great and good.'"

Fitzgerald witnessed one of Washington's greatest moments in battle. *The Catholic World* describes it as "the most graphic incident of Fitzgerald's connection with the great commander." The incident in question, a scene at the battle of Princeton, was described by George Washington Parke Custis, the adopted son of Washington, in his memoirs: "We have often enjoyed a touching reminiscence of that ever memorable event from the late Colonel Fitzgerald, who was aide to the chief, and who never related the story of his general's danger without adding to his story the homage of a tear."

Washington's army, between Trenton and Princeton, encountered two British battalions and the fighting was fierce. The Americans were being driven back until Washington urged his steed forward to better direct his army's musket fire. Washington was now out in front of his men and a despairing Fitzgerald watched as the bullets flew closer. Finally, Fitzgerald could take it no more and, convinced Washington would be shot by either friendly fire or British muskets, buried his face in his hat, unable to watch.

He was aroused a few moments later by Washington riding up to him unscathed. The tough young Irishman broke down in tears . . . Washington smiled and grasped his young friend's hand and simply said, "The day is ours."

Griffin adds an interesting addendum: "At the critical moment of the retreat of Mercer's men, and when Washington was rallying the stricken force, John Mullowney, a Philadelphia Catholic boy, a drummer with the Philadelphia militia, 'pounded out Yankee Doodle' with so much spirit and force that the waning courage of the soldiers revived and forced the British to retreat. He afterwards became an officer of the Navy under Commodore John Barry."

It was Colonel Fitzgerald who gladly informed a deeply relieved Mrs. Washington that her husband had triumphed at Trenton and Princeton.

After the war, Fitzgerald was one of four men chosen by Washington as board members of his Potomac Company to create a new channel for the Potomac River, which would greatly expedite the passage of goods.

The two men continued to be close. Griffin notes that:

> Saint Patrick's Day, 1788, was also election day in Virginia for the choice of delegates to the State Convention, which should ratify or reject the Federal Constitution proposed at Philadelphia in 1787. Washington came from Mount Vernon to vote for candidates in its favor; and Colonel Fitzgerald entertained him at a dinner party, to which some of the principal inhabitants of the town were invited.
>
> July 4, 1799, Independence Day was celebrated in Alexandria. Washington was present, and, after Colonel Fitzgerald had "put the military commands through the manual, Washington expressed his satisfaction with their military and elegant appearance."
>
> Aug. 7, 1799, Colonel Fitzgerald dined with Washington, and in November of the same year the General visited Alexandria on business and dined at the city hotel with Fitzgerald.

It was his last public appearance beyond Mount Vernon. In the early winter of 1799, Washington died. John Fitzgerald followed soon after. As Griffin notes: "He is buried in the Catholic cemetery of Alexandria, on the road to Mount Vernon, the home of his General and the resting place of his remains."

As always, he is in sight of his leader.

CHAPTER 7

The Irish Patriot Who Invented the Name "United States of America"

At the beginning of 1776, Stephen Moylan, Cork-born aide-de-camp to General George Washington, wrote to Joseph Reed, Washington's military secretary, with a request to be made an ambassador to Spain where he had family. After all his service to Washington, he felt this would be a deserved posting.

In the process, he gave birth to a new title for the country he and Washington had served so well: "I would vastly like to go with full and ample powers from the *United States of America* to Spain."

It was the first time the "United States of America" name was used as the title for the new country that was being born through revolution and strife.

As Erin Allen notes on the Library of Congress blog, America was named after an Italian explorer: "While the colonies may have established it, America was given a name long before. America is named after Amerigo Vespucci, the Italian explorer who set forth the then revolutionary concept that the lands that Christopher Columbus sailed to in 1492 were part of a separate continent. A map created in 1507 by Martin Waldseemüller was the first to depict this new continent with the name 'America,' a Latinized version of Amerigo."

The impact of Moylan's reference was immediate. Jefferson used the phrase in the Declaration of Independence and others are certainly on the record as using it in and around June 1776.

But the New York Historical Society proved without a shadow of a doubt that it was the Irish Catholic Moylan, as far back as January 2, 1776, who coined the phrase which would become the name of the most powerful nation on earth.

The Moylan letter was discovered around Memorial Day 2013 and was greeted with disbelief by many who wanted it to be the invention of Jefferson, of Thomas Paine, or of Washington himself.

Yet there it is, contained in Moylan's letter, used for the first recorded time on January 2, 1776.

In retrospect, however, Moylan was no obscure figure who stumbled across what would become the famous name of the country he served.

The closeness of his relationship to Washington was referred to upon his passing on April 13, 1811. *Claypole's American Daily Advertiser* wrote a detailed tribute which included the following information: "He served with distinction in the American Army during the whole of the war and he enjoyed a larger share of the favor and friendship of the Revolutionary War Commander in Chief . . . a decisive proof . . . of the elevation of his character and the merits of his service."

The high regard Washington held for Moylan was also evident when he hired him as secretary and aide-de-camp. His description of the kind of deputy he needed as war broke out is contained in a letter to a friend:

> The business, as I hinted to you before, is considerably Increased, by being more comprehensive; and, at this time (from the great changes which have, and are happening every day) perplexed; so that you would want a good Writer, and a Methodical Man, as he should be a person in whose Integrity you can confide, and on whose capacity—care—& method you can rely. At present, my time is so much taken

up at my Desk, that I am obliged to neglect many other essential parts of my Duty; it is absolutely necessary therefore for me to have persons that can think for me, as well as execute Orders.

Moylan was the choice.

After a later promotion for Moylan, Washington made his approval known: "I have the pleasure to inform you that he is now appointed. I have no doubt from your account of this gentleman of his discharging the duty with honor and fidelity."

How did this unknown Irish Catholic find his way to George Washington's side and win his trust and confidence to the point where, despite occasional disputes, they created an amazing friendship and working team?

Actually, it all starts with the British-imposed Penal Laws on Ireland in an attempt to obliterate the Catholic religion. After Oliver Cromwell, on a murderous rampage through Ireland, had done his worst from 1649 to 1653 to exterminate the Irish people, a set of draconian laws were put in place designed to kill off Irish Catholicism forever.

Known as the Penal Laws, they especially focused on ending Catholic worship, work prospects, and education. One of the most punitive stated: "If any Papist shall publicly teach schools or instruct youth in learning in any private house or shall be entertained to instruct youth he shall incur such penalties and forfeitures as any Popish regular is liable to."

Essentially, this particular Penal Law meant Irish Catholics caught practicing their faith would be jailed and forfeit land and even their lives if they continued.

According to Edmund Burke, the Penal Laws were "a machine of wise and elaborate contrivance, as well fitted for the oppression, impoverishment and degradation of a people, and the debasement in them of human nature itself, as ever proceeded from the perverted ingenuity of man."

But they did not succeed in extirpating the Irish.

According to a writer called John Hugh Campbell, in his book on the *History of the Hibernian Society and the Friendly Sons of Saint Patrick* (an organization of Irish professionals founded in Philadelphia in 1771, which Moylan chaired when it was founded), Stephen Moylan was part of a relatively prosperous merchant family in Cork from his birth in 1737.

Moylan was one of eight children and was from a devout Catholic family—one sister became a nun and a brother, Francis, became a priest and later Bishop of Cork.

But education was impossible in the Penal Law era and Stephen Moylan, like so many children of well-to-do Catholic merchants, was sent abroad to study, in his case to France. Campbell's history records that Moylan and his brother were smuggled out of the country. There is evidence to suggest that he was educated by the Jesuits in France.

France, at the time, was entering the enlightenment phase and writers like Voltaire, Diderot, and Rousseau were inspiring revolutionary thinking about the inequities of the state under the monarchy. Moylan became a fierce advocate of freedom and equality as a result, a fact that became evident in his enthusiasm to begin the war against the British on behalf of the colonies after he moved to the United States.

Before that move, Moylan and his brother seem to have moved from France to Lisbon, where they founded a successful shipping company.

Stephen Moylan came to America at age thirty-one in 1768, and took up residence in Philadelphia. He arrived as a man of means, and was soon a well-respected business leader.

He entered the shipping business and also land speculation. In an advertisement dated March 23, 1768, two thousand acres of land in Morris County, New Jersey were put on sale fifteen miles from Newark and described as being located in as "as healthy a county as any in the world." Among those to whom inquiries should be made was Stephen Moylan.

Evidence of Moylan's social status and prosperity was also noted in 1770 when he became a member of the Gloucester Fox Hunting Club where he had a reputation as a magnificent horseman.

Despite moving three thousand miles away, Moylan was not about to forget his roots and the savage suffering of the Irish people under the Penal Laws.

On March 17, 1771, the Friendly Sons of Saint Patrick organization was formed in Philadelphia and was composed mostly of "prosperous merchants." Twenty-four people were signed up and Moylan became the first president.

The organization's stated aim was raising funds for poor Irish immigrants. Moylan was one of three Catholics out of the twenty-four members. There would be no religious distinction—"the spirit of liberality and justice ever pervaded," according to historian Martin Griffin.

He remained a constant presence in the Friendly Sons, welcoming Washington as an honored guest and stepping down as president in 1773 when he was noted as being "beyond seas."

In 1774, he is even mentioned in the diary of future president John Adams as having dined with him and Richard Penn, a sure sign of regard and influence. Most importantly, there was also General Charles Lee, Washington's future second in command of the Continental Army, so clearly Moylan was considered a major figure.

In 1775, the inevitable war had come. The Continental Congress met on May 10, 1775, to officially launch the battle for self-rule and freedom from the British.

George Washington was elected commander in chief. The revolution had begun, and Moylan was determined not to miss it.

Leading Philadelphia lawyer John Dickinson, a huge figure in Patriot circles and a close friend of both Moylan and Washington, urgently recommended Moylan to Washington. Dickinson's letter read: "Mr Moylan, a friend of mine, informs me that he intends to enter the American army. He is much esteemed here. I am convinced he will endeavor to deserve [hiring]."

Washington replied: "I have the pleasure to inform you that [Moylan] is now appointed Commissary of Musters [essentially quartermaster, a vital position]. I have no doubt he will discharge the duty with honor and fidelity."

The army he joined was ill-fitted for purpose, as his associate and close friend Joseph Reed stated in a letter that he sent: "We [Reed and Moylan] heard, and we find it true, that the army was a sea of disorder and confusion, that the officers were not only ignorant and litigious but scandalously disobedient, and in the last action many of them proved such notorious cowards that the very existence of the army, and consequently the salvation of America, depended upon an immediate reform."

In the letter, Reed stated that Washington was at a breaking point trying to create a professional army and, were it not for men like Moylan and Reed, the army would have collapsed. Reed stated: "I thought myself bound by every tie of duty and honor to comply with his [Washington's] request to help him through his sea of difficulties."

As the war began, Moylan's maritime experience resulted in Washington asking Moylan to intercept two ships from Britain loaded with "arms, powder and other stores" bound for Quebec.

Moylan and Colonel John Glover of the Marine regiment were put in charge of the interception. They succeeded in fitting two ships but delays in sailing, because of various difficulties, prevented the interception.

It was emblematic of the naval crisis Washington faced. As the war progressed, it became evident that Britain easily controlled the high seas and the coastlines as the Americans scrambled to put together a naval force. After their shock defeat in Boston, the British readied an armada of 160 ships in Nova Scotia, ready to sail to New York to bring a swift end to the revolution.

It seemed pre-ordained. Time and again, with fully gunned and manned vessels and centuries of experience behind them, the British faced no serious opposition from an American navy that was non-existent. The truth was that Washington did not have a single ship to confront the armada.

Washington's decision to blunt the naval advantage and try and defeat the British as they came ashore on Long Island, before they gained a toehold, failed miserably, and his men were soon on the run. Moylan, as a chief organizer of supply lines and setting up sea barriers to the British advance, found his task utterly impossible and the British flooded almost unimpeded into New York. It was Moylan's lowest hour and he resigned his commission, intending instead to join Washington's inner circle as an aide and volunteer. He even had to survive a court martial as the blame game intensified.

Washington, while initially angry, never lost faith in his Irish protégé.

Due to his skill as a horseman, Moylan was placed in charge of the Fourth Continental Light Dragoons.

His troopers were unmistakable—on their fiery steeds they were decked in green. It was the glory days of cavalry and Moylan was the swashbuckling leader as his dragoons slashed at the enemies' flanks in battle after battle. Moylan's men became so successful in harrying the British that a well-known song was composed about him and his men.

His greatest moment came in the final act of the Revolutionary War at Yorktown when his company, also known as the Green Islanders, performed brilliantly. They also played a key role in securing the January 1777 victory at Princeton, which motivated Moylan to write to Robert Morris, a financier of the revolution.

Speaking of Washington, Moylan wrote: "By heavens it was the best piece of generalship I ever heard of or read . . . I have never felt like one of Homer's Deities before. We trod on air—it was a glorious day . . . How your heart went pitpat, when that news reached you, and what an agreeable feeling you must all have had when you heard. . ."

On Saint Patrick's Day, 1784, Moylan was present and in the company of Commodore John Barry, the Irish-born founder of the US Navy.

By then, Moylan was a major figure due to his proximity to Washington.

The song "Moylan's Dragoons" was supposedly sung after the victory at Yorktown:

Moylan's Dragoons
Fuel up the banner of the brave.

And bear it gently home,
No more o'er Moylan's march to wave.
Lodge it in Moylan's home.
There Butler, Hand, and Wayne, perchance,
May tell of battle's o'er,
And the old flag, on its splinter's lance,
Unfurl for joy once more.

Thus was Stephen Moylan remembered in the popular ballad that bore his name. He went on to serve in the Virginia legislature and was a highly successful businessman. Now he will be forever known as the creator of the name the "United States of America" for the dawning Republic for which he fought so hard. He died in April 1811, aged seventy-four.

CHAPTER 8

Timothy Murphy Fires the Shot that Changed America

In 1929, New York Governor Franklin Delano Roosevelt attended the dedication of a monument in Saratoga, New York to the memory of Timothy Murphy, frontiersman, controversial Native American fighter, and American patriot.

He was also very likely the man who fired the shot that changed American history at the Battle of Saratoga in October 1777.

At the dedication of the memorial to Murphy, the governor of New York said:

> This country has been made by the Timothy Murphys, the men in the ranks. Conditions here called for qualities of heart and hand that Tim Murphy had in abundance. Our histories should tell us more about the men in the ranks, for it was to them, more than to the generals, that we were indebted for our military victories.

Murphy had indeed been in the ranks from Valley Forge to Yorktown as he soldiered with Washington, and numerous battles in between. He was known as "Sure Shot" because of his uncanny aim with a rifle, which was a new-fangled invention vastly superior in accuracy to the musket. He became an elite sharpshooter and a member of General Daniel Morgan's sniper division.

He would end up as something more than an ordinary soldier, though, despite Roosevelt's description of him. To this very day, he is a subject of controversy and still well remembered in Schoharie County, New York, where he eventually settled. There is a monument to him in the cemetery of the town of Middleburgh and an annual ten thousand meter race that bears his name. He died of cancer in 1816. He was illiterate all his life, but was considered one of the ablest soldiers in the revolutionary army.

Timothy Murphy was born in 1751 near the Delaware Water Gap in Pennsylvania. His parents, Thomas and Mary Murphy, emigrated from Donegal to find a new life in America. Timothy moved twice, ending up in Wyoming County, Pennsylvania right on the edge of the then-western frontier.

A warrior from his earliest days, Timothy Murphy became a legendary Native American fighter and later a soldier in the Continental Army. The evidence indicates he fired what is often considered one of the most important shots of the American Revolution on October 7, 1777.

More than 220 years later, the question of who killed the British General Simon Fraser, who was waging a magnificent battle against the Patriot army at the second battle of Saratoga, is unresolved, but Murphy is considered far more likely than anyone else to have taken down Fraser.

The shot turned the tide for the Americans at a time they desperately needed help and, most importantly, it convinced the French it was time to join in as American allies. Saratoga was the turning point in the war.

George Washington realized how vital the victory was, declaring a day of Thanksgiving on December 18, 1777, to celebrate the victory.

Benjamin Franklin, the envoy to France, also seized the chance to convince the dubious French that the Americans would be a powerful ally and that joining with them made military sense.

Murphy was a legendary figure long before he enlisted in the fight. Nowadays, his actions in the wars would be considered savage and bloodthirsty. The ambition of men like Murphy and his cohorts were simple. Rid the American territories of the Native Americans forever. The fact that the Native Americans had entered a pact with the British against the Patriots made the hatred and desire to vanquish even more compelling on both sides.

Murphy soon became known as the chief Native American fighter on the frontier but also stood out for his viciousness in battle.

A biography by William Sigsby, written in 1836, portrayed Murphy as every bit a bloodthirsty killer in his own way as any Native American ever was alleged to be.

Sisgby wrote: "Sometimes [Murphy] habited in the dress of the Indian, with his face painted, he would pass among them, making important discoveries as to their strength and designs without detection."

Sigsby also relates some of Murphy's infamous brutality during a hand-to-hand fight: "The Indian was very large and powerful and Murphy being exceedingly angry, skinned his legs and drew it over his long stockings . . . But the skin of the Indian having shrunk, began to gall his legs, whereupon he took his hunting knife and ripped them off."

Murphy scalped and tomahawked his victims in the name of frontier justice.

Sigsby's description of Murphy destroying a Native American village in a midnight raid once the warriors had left to go hunting (so only the old and very young and women were left) makes tough reading.

He writes:

At one time Murphy and a small body of riflemen were despatched to destroy an Indian and Tory village near Unadilla. After a laborious march through marshes and over mountains in which they endured innumerable privations, they arrived in sight of the village, which lay in a beautiful valley.

They remained on the mountain until midnight, when they advanced slowly and cautiously. Luckily most of the Indians were absent, and after a warm contest, in which clubs, fists, feet and tomahawks were used by the old Indians, squaws and papooses, and were resented by the riflemen with fists, feet and the ends of their guns, the village was reduced to ashes.

Despite such actions along the way, he became a folk hero figure. The statue to him in upstate New York in Middleburgh Cemetery near Schenectady depicts a man in frontiersman garb, rifle in hand, and a Cherokee Native American's skull lying at the base of the statue.

It is always unwise to project a later generation's views on the behavior of previous generations, particularly with regard to situations such as the treatment of Native Americans, but there is little doubt it was kill or be killed, and the more savage the better back in the frontier days. By siding with the British, the tribes had ensured that conflict with the patriot army would ensue.

As is clear from the three monuments to him, the dispute over his viciousness to Native Americans, or whether or not he fired the shot that killed Fraser, has not stopped the veneration of Timothy Murphy by others.

The Ancient Order of Hibernians mounted a memorial to Murphy on the Saratoga battlefield where they say his great deed was accomplished. In 2002, a ceremony was held by the Hibernians, headed by local president Chris Mills. Mills stated correctly, "It was on this ground that a nation was born," and added that Murphy had played a major role.

On June 29, 1775, right after the Revolutionary War began, Murphy enlisted and was immediately catapulted into battle, including on Long Island. He later wintered at Valley Forge and fought at the battles of Trenton, Princeton, and Yorktown.

Murphy was a valuable recruit noted as being an "expert marksman" (described as being "able to hit a seven-inch target at 250 yards") which made him a natural for General Daniel Morgan's new strike force called "Morgan's Riflemen."

In 1777, he was selected as one of five hundred handpicked rifle-men to go with General Morgan to upstate New York to help stop the advance south into the Hudson River Valley of General John Burgoyne and the British Army.

Burgoyne was a supremely overconfident general who believed strongly in the superiority of British fighting skills. Historian George Billias described him as "a buffoon in uniform who bungled his assignments badly."

The British plan in 1777 was to trap the American army at Saratoga with Burgoyne and the armies of Generals William Howe and Henry Clinton applying the coup de grace to the pesky Americans in a massive pincer movement, with Howe coming east, Clinton north from New York, and Burgoyne south.

But terrible communications and sheer incompetence saw Burgoyne face the Americans alone. It would prove the turning point of the Revolutionary War. The British also learned that, far from being a ragtag army, the Americans could fight.

History awaited Timothy Murphy, too, at Saratoga. He had joined Captain Daniel Morgan's army rifle unit, who were sent to Saratoga as the American snipers of their day.

The new-fangled rifle was far more accurate from long range than the musket but took too much time to load and had such a thin barrel that no bayonet could be affixed to it. As most battles ended up in close quarters, bayonets were incredibly important.

Thus, riflemen became the original US Army sniper group, tak-ing part in specific engagements where long range shooting ability was a key factor in a battle; across a field, say, rather than a forest. The rifle could land a hit at three hundred yards; the range of a mus-ket was eighty yards at best.

The riflemen had to display extreme accuracy before being accepted by Morgan. One contemporary account in a Virginia newspaper reported on an exhibition the riflemen held: "A man held between his knees a board 5 inches wide and seven inches long, with a paper bulls-eye the size of a dollar. A rifleman at 60 yards without a rest, put eight bullets in succession through the bulls-eye."

From the same source we are told that the rifleman gave an exhibition "in which a company, on a quick advance, placed their shots in 7 inch targets at 250 yards."

On October 7, 1777, as the second battle of Saratoga rolled on, the British sought to make a breakthrough (which could well have ended the Revolutionary War) by cutting off the northern states from their southern cohorts, leaving the Continental Army hopelessly divided.

At the first Battle of Saratoga a few weeks earlier, it was American riflemen who prevented a massive defeat by aiming withering fire at British officers who were decked out in finery different from their enlisted men and thus easy targets.

The second battle was also saved by the marksmen and, ironically, Benedict Arnold, who led his men in a frenzied charge to force the British back just as they looked likely to cut though the American line. Arnold had fallen out with US Commander Howard Gates, who wished to wage a far more cautious war. He forbade Arnold from taking to the field, an order Arnold ignored. Arnold had the troops firmly behind him.

Murphy, the sniper, believed that Arnold would never have turned traitor were it not for the failure to properly congratulate and credit him on his battle-saving charge, a belief shared by all the enlisted men. Instead, the official kudos went to the general in charge, the British-born Gates, who was later to prove a disastrous leader known as the "Coward of Camden" when he ran from a southern battle in the Carolinas.

A major turning point in the second battle of Saratoga was the shooting of British Brigadier General Simon Fraser by one of Morgan's snipers from a great distance. Time and again, Fraser had rallied his men and threatened to turn the tide of battle. Morgan called out loudly for him to be shot. How exactly it happened is lost to the mists of time. In 1853, a letter by a British officer, written four days after the battle, shed some light on how Fraser died. The officer stated he had talked directly to Morgan and Morgan told him how Fraser's death had happened: Morgan said, "I saw that they were led by an officer on a grey horse—a devilish brave fellow; so, when we took the height a second time, said I to one of my best shots, said I, you get up into that tree, and single him out on the white horse. Dang it, 'twas no sooner said than done. On came the British again, with the grey horseman leading; but his career was short enough this time. I just took my eyes off him for a moment, when I turned them to the place where he had been—pooh, he was gone!"

Years later, historian N. C. Brooks wrote a magazine article naming Murphy and adding information about the weapon without citing a source. An 1827 account written by Samuel Woodruff, Esq., of Windsor, Connecticut also came to light. He was an actual participant in the battle.

He witnessed Morgan ordering "his riflemen" to specifically target General Fraser. Woodruff added:

. . . the crupper of the grey horse was cut off by a rifle bullet, and within the next minute another passed through the horse's mane, a little back of his ears. An aid [sic] of Fraser, noticing this, observed to him, "Sir, it is evident that you are marked out for a particular aim; would it not be prudent for you to retire from this place?" Fraser replied, "my duty forbids me to fly from danger," and immediately received a bullet through his body.

Woodruff does not indicate a source of this information nor mention any rifleman's name.

Historian William Stone echoes this and credits Murphy directly with the hit:

Within a few moments a rifle ball cut the crouper of Fraser's horse, and another passed through his horse's mane. Calling his attention to this, Fraser's aide said, "It is evident that you are marked out for a particular aim; would it not be prudent for you to retire from this place?" Fraser replied, "my duty forbids me to fly from danger." The next moment he fell mortally wounded by a ball from the rifle of Murphy.

There are various estimates that the shot that took down Fraser came from three hundred to five hundred yards away, an astonishing hit. There is also ample evidence that Murphy was the shooter. But some argue that Morgan would have asked more than one rifleman to take a shot at the British brigadier who was looking more and more likely to turn the tide of the battle,

Stone also noted that Charles Neilson, whose father fought at Saratoga, said: "The soldier who shot General Fraser was Timothy Murphy, a Virginian, who belonged to Morgan's rifle corps." Another historian, Benjamin Silliman, made a visit to the battlefield in 1820, and wrote:

> The following anecdote, related to me at Ballston Springs, in 1797, by the Hon. Richard Brent, then a member of Congress, from Virginia, who derived the fact from General Morgan's own mouth.
>
> Colonel Morgan took a few of his best riflemen aside; men in whose fidelity, and fatal precision of aim, he could repose the most perfect confidence, and said to them: "that gallant officer is General Fraser; I admire and respect him, but it is necessary that he should die—take your stations in that wood and do your duty." Within a few moments General Fraser fell, mortally wounded.

Historian Don Higginbotham, on the other hand, says Murphy's weapon was a double-barrel rifle.

We will never know for certain who shot the bullet that changed the Battle of Saratoga, but it is fair to say that Murphy's name is the only one associated with the kill. There is no doubt Morgan wanted Fraser shot down and it's very likely that more than one sharpshooter tried but that Murphy was certainly involved, as well as being the most likely shooter.

After the war, Murphy settled down. His first wife, Peggy (née Margaret Feeck), was the daughter of Johannes Feeck, a prosperous Dutch farmer in Schoharie Valley in central New York. Timothy and Margaret Murphy had five sons and four daughters.

Following the 1807 death of his first wife, Murphy remarried Mary Robertson and relocated with her to Charlottesville. He had four more sons. Murphy is considered a hero in Schoharie County, New York where he resided. As I previously shared, in the cemetery in Middleburgh, a monument has been erected and an annual walk is named in his honor.

Timothy Murphy, an illiterate Irish American, has gone down in history as the most likely person to have changed the course of the Second Battle of Saratoga while living up to his nickname "Sure Shot." His aim changed the course of the battle that changed the course of the war.

Washington Saves Saint Patrick's Day Twice

We will learn George Washington's stance on Irish Catholics at a time of great oppression. The only Catholic to sign the Declaration of Independence was also the richest man in America.

CHAPTER 9

Dramatic Saint Patrick's Days as Washington Proudly Wears the Green

"May the generous Sons of Saint Patrick expel all the venomous reptiles of Britain."

—George Washington, June 1776,
drinking a toast to the Irish as reported by
the *New-York Gazette* and the
New-York Packet newspapers

George Washington was all in on the Irish struggle for freedom. As the Mount Vernon Historical record notes: "General Washington, and the larger American population, was fascinated by the mounting political unrest in Ireland . . . Ireland's patriotic struggle against the British crown mirrored their own hunger for liberty."

Washington's warm feelings for the Irish and the influence of the Irish fight for independence showed themselves in several ways.

He clearly believed his own words that the Irish had a "firm adherence . . . to the glorious cause in which we are embarked."

He did not have to look hard for evidence of that.

According to *Smithsonian Magazine*, the Sons of Saint Patrick's toast was a clever call. "Generals born in Ireland or who had Irish parents commanded seven of the eleven brigades wintering in Morristown," the magazine notes—a figure that makes entirely clear how important Irish leaders and men were in the vanguard.

What also drew Washington to the Irish was the fact that in Ireland there was enormous support for the Americans fighting the same hated British for their freedom. The Lord Lieutenant of Ireland from 1776 to 1780, John Hobart, Earl of Buckinghamshire, wrote that the Irish Presbyterians were "in their hearts Americans" and they were "talking in all companies in such a way that if they are not rebels, it is hard to find a name for them."

Two separate Saint Patrick's Day events in 1778 and 1779 also make Washington's feelings clear. In the vast encampment at Valley Forge in the winter of 1777 and the spring of 1778, the eleven thousand soldiers of the Continental Army under George Washington suffered great deprivation, as did the five hundred domestic women camp followers.

It was not so much from the weather, which had none of the savagery that the winter of 1778 would have, but the fact that so many were ill clad, without shoes, and there were constant interruptions in the food supply. Men were surly, quick to see insult, and fearful of what lay ahead. There were rumors of mutiny, as there would be again.

If an army marches on its stomach, as Napoleon would later claim, then Washington's men had empty bellies and were in dire danger of taking Napoleon's future edict to the extreme. Food was a constant source of anxiety and fretfulness.

As Saint Patrick's Day, March 17, approached, the tensions between different ethnic groups within Washington's army rose like the spring tides.

The Pennsylvania Germans, in particular, loved to ruffle the Irish battalions. Germany had sent the most participants of any European group, outside the British and Irish, into battle during the Revolutionary War.

German soldiers served in equal numbers in both armies, while there were many Germans associated with pacifism rather than fighting.

That dislike of battle did not extend to members of Washington's German battalions. The Germans were quite frequently recruited into what would now be known as the military police.

As such, they were often the guards and captors of soldiers who had broken the law in some way, either through drinking, scuffling, or more serious deeds. The Irish, with their love of carousing, were obvious offenders.

The Germans were known as rough jailers; they also stood apart as very few Germans knew the English language, which almost all of the army spoke, which led to numerous misunderstandings and conflicts.

There was bad blood from the beginning with Washington's Irish battalions, likely due to German hostility to the rule-bending Irish. On one infamous occasion, it almost spilled over into all-out battle.

As remembered by Colonel Allan McLane of the Continental Army, Washington himself had to get personally involved to resolve the matter. McLane wrote the following account in the wake of the incident, the text of which is contained in the annals of the Pennsylvania Historical Society:

When Washington and his army lay at Valley Forge in 1778 some of the Pennsylvania Germans made a Paddy and displayed it on Saint Patrick's Day to the great indignation of the Irish in the camp. [A scarecrow covered with flecks of green cloth and a bishop's mitre on its head. Basically, it's a Protestant insult to St. Patrick and the Irish.]

They [the Irish] assembled in large bodies under arms, swearing for vengeance against the New England troops saying they had got up [created] the insult. The affair threatened [to become] a very serious issue; none of the officers could appease them.

At this, Washington, having ascertained the entire innocence [according to themselves] of the [German] troops rode up to the Irish and kindly and feelingly argued with them, and then requested the Irish to show the offenders and he would see them punished.

They could not designate anyone. "Well," said Washington, with great promptness, "I too am a great lover of Saint Patrick's Day, and must settle the affair by making all the army celebrate the day."

He therefore ordered extra drink to every man of his command and thus all made merry and were good friends.

It is clear from the account that Washington sided with the Irish and called for a party in their honor.

A year later, it was very different. The camp was at Jockey Hollow in Morristown, New Jersey, not far from Valley Forge, and it was a cold coming that greeted the Continental Army when they took to their winter quarters.

Twenty-eight separate snowstorms raged down on the shivering army between November 1779 and April 1780. Snow drifts of six feet were common. It was the coldest winter ever measured up to that time.

It was the cruelest time of the American Revolution. Men froze to death while others crowded together for warmth and survival. Food was scarce and disease rampant. The dreaded smallpox made its appearance, thankfully stymied by vaccines. But it still left many men weak and ailing. It was the ultimate winter of discontent. There was renewed talk of mutiny.

How bad was it at Morristown? "We were absolutely, literally starved," Private Joseph Plumb Martin recalled after the war. "I do solemnly declare that I did not put a single morsel of victuals into my mouth for four days and as many nights, except a little black birch bark which I gnawed off a stick of wood, if that can be called victuals. I saw several of the men roast their old shoes and eat them, and I was afterwards informed by one of the officers' waiters, that some of the officers killed and ate a favorite little dog that belonged to one of them."

By March, the storms and the snow drifts had not let up or disappeared. Washington sought for a way to keep morale up. He decided to give his entire army a day off, on Saint Patrick's Day, March 17.

It was testament to thousands of Irish who fought for him that Washington decided Saint Patrick's Day would be the only day of the year to offer his men a surcease and bring some lightness of spirit amid the encircling gloom.

As for his part, Washington was captivated by the Irish struggle being fought by the United Irishmen with the same ideals and vision that Washington had of true freedoms for all.

So it was no surprise that Washington decided that Saint Patrick's Day 1780 would be a day of rest and revelry—an occasion to express solidarity with the "brave and generous" people of Ireland.

Washington issued the following proclamation: "The General directs that all fatigue and working parties cease for to-morrow the SEVENTEENTH instant," read the orders, "a day held in particular regard by the people of [Ireland]."

Washington also asked "that the celebration of the day will not be attended with the least rioting or disorder."

Washington himself personally celebrated. The *New Jersey Journal,* in its issue of March 15, 1780, published an account of a dinner in the camp at Morristown the day before:

"An elegant collation [meal] was provided by the officers of Colonel Jackson's regiment" which Washington and several of his staff attended. Thirteen toasts were drunk, among them "St Patrick: The Volunteer of Ireland: May the cannons of Ireland bellow until the nation be free," as well as toasts to the Irish leaders at the time who had won their own parliament (The Act of Union dissolved it in 1800), Henry Grattan, and the Duke of Leinster.

The *New-York Gazette* reports that "next morning was ushered in with music and the hoisting of colors exhibiting the 13 stripes, the favorite harp and an inscription reading in capitals 'The Independence of Ireland.'"

Washington issued a further proclamation about Ireland on March 16: "The General congratulates the army and the very interesting proceedings of the parliament and the inhabitants of the country which have lately been communicated not only as they appear calculated to remove those heavy and tyrannical oppression . . . but to restore to a brave and generous people their ancient rights and freedoms."

As a shrewd commander, Washington knew that paying tribute to the fight for Irish freedom would play very well with his Irish troops. Luke Gardner, a member of the Irish parliament, stated in the Irish House of Commons in 1784 that he had been told "it was a common practice for the soldiers of the Pennsylvania line to converse in the Irish language."

Light-Horse Harry Lee, father of Confederate general Robert E. Lee, wrote in his memoir about the Pennsylvania battalion: "They were known by the designation of The Line of Pennsylvania but they should have been called the 'Line of Ireland.'"

Lee the senior was especially close to Washington, eulogizing him when he died as "first in war, first in peace and first in the hearts of his countrymen." No doubt his respect for the Irish was shared by Washington.

In a biography of Commodore John Barry, the Irish-born founder of the American navy, author Joseph Gurn highlights how dear Ireland remained to Barry and all Irish fighting in the Revolutionary War and recounts the following story from an officer:

> While the army lay at Valley Forge in December 1776, Major Forest, in compliance with a regular order, marched the officers of his Irish regiment to take the oath to defend and support the independence of the United States.
>
> An Irish officer stepping forward exclaimed "Before we go in could you not, major, contrive to see the general and prevail upon him to put little Ireland in the oath?"
>
> "That we could never do," replied the major, "but while we are engaged with England on the one side, let Ireland seize the golden opportunity and assail her on the other. Now is the time."

Washington was completely aware of the drive for freedom in Ireland.

As for the number of Irish in Washington's army, the redoubtable Irish American historian Michael O'Brien in his 1937 book, *George Washington's Associations with the Irish,* counted more than ten thousand Irish names among the enlistment rolls kept by Washington of recruits to the Continental Army across the full period of the war.

(It should be noted that St Patrick's Day was celebrated rather differently among the Irish fighting for the British. As the *Journal of The Friendly Sons of Saint Patrick* noted: "'Volunteers of Ireland', enlisted on the royal side of the dispute, [sat] down 400 strong on March 17, 1779, to a banquet in the Bowery where the King, no doubt, was toasted while the 'shamrock was drowned.' These Volunteers a year later were deserting to the patriots in such numbers that Lord Rawdon was offering '10 guineas for the head of any deserter.'" It was obvious where Irish sympathies lay, even at the heart of the British Army.)

CHAPTER 10

Washington's Inner Irish Circle Revealed

Though anti-Catholicism and anti-Irish sentiment was rampant in the colonies, George Washington paid little heed to such prejudices.

There is extensive written testimony from the man himself, and among the diaries of others, that he bore no ill will toward Irish Catholics, unlike so many of his contemporaries.

Washington's embrace of the Irish, both privately and publicly, was extremely unusual for its time when anti-Irish Catholic feelings were widespread.

As the First Amendment Encyclopedia notes, his writings are remarkably free of religious prejudice. In a letter seeking workers for his estate in 1784, for example, he remarked: "If they are good workmen, they may be of Asia, Africa, or Europe. They may be Momometans, Jews or Christians of any Sect, or they may be Atheists."

It is clear from his own writings that, unlike so many in his time, he was devoid of anti-Catholic bigotry. He was never heard to question a man's religion and he frequently attended Roman Catholic masses. On Sunday, October 9, 1774, for instance, he attended mass at Saint Mary's Church in the town of Spruce, near Philadelphia. He noted in his diary that he had attended the "Romish" church which was a term widely used at the time and was not considered derogatory.

"Went in the afternoon to the Romish church and heard a good disclosure about parents upon their duties to their children founded in justice and charity. The scenery and the music are so calculated to take mankind that I wonder if the reformation ever succeeded. The paintings, the bells, the candles, the gold and silver, our Savior on the cross over the latter at full length the chanting is exquisitely soft and sweet."

He was outspoken against religious bigotry against Catholics. As historian Michael O'Brien relates, some Protestant soldiers were about to celebrate "Pope Day" which consisted of the burning of an effigy of the pontiff during the siege of Boston in 1775.

Washington immediately admonished them. Writing in the third person, he stated: "The Commander in Chief has been apprised of a [scheme] formed for that ridiculous and childish custom of burning the effigy of the pope. He cannot help but be surprised that there should be officers and soldiers in this army so void of common sense as not to see the [foolishness] of such a step at this Juncture."

He was not himself overly religious. He believed in providence, that mysterious helping hand that reached out to aid him at key moments, but did not single out just one religion to follow. Instead, he believed all should be treated equally and allowed to practice and their followers should be allowed to work free from prejudice.

His particular attitude to Catholicism was best expressed in a letter to future traitor Benedict Arnold as the latter prepared to leave with an expeditionary force to go to Canada where the majority of the citizens were Catholic.

Washington said Arnold's army was "to avoid all Disrespect to or Contempt of the Religion of a Country by ridiculing any of its Ceremonies or affronting its ministers or Votaries . . . you are to be particularly careful to restrain every officer and soldier from such folly and to punish every instance of it.

"On the other hand, so far as it lies in your power you are to protect and support the free exercise of religion of the country and the undisturbed enjoyment of the rights of conscience in religious matters with your utter influence and authority."

Washington's benign view of the Catholic religion encouraged Irish who joined up that they felt no prejudice from the top. Historian Michael O'Brien was steadfast in his conviction that there were far more Irish Catholics involved with Washington in the revolution than has been conceded, and that the acceptance of their religion by Washington played a part in recruiting Irish soldiers. The lack of anti-Catholic prejudice meant the Irish were even more ready to fight for him.

The Marquis de Chastellux, a high ranking member of the French military forces fighting with the Americans, wrote that the Irish were especially committed to the war, in his estimation.

As relayed by historian Philip Thomas Tucker in his book, *How the Irish Won the American Revolution*, De Chastellux wrote: "An Irishman the instant he sets foot on American soil becomes . . . an American. This was uniformly the case during the whole of the [American Revolution]. While Englishmen and Scotchmen were treated with jealousy and distrust, a native of Ireland stood in need of no other certificate than his [brogue]."

Revolutionary War historian Thomas Fleming stated that one of the greatest surprises he encountered when doing his research was just how many Irish were at Valley Forge then. The numbers were much higher than historians have allowed.

So Washington's overtures to the Irish and his bond with them was well worth the effort. Nonetheless, it was highly unusual for a scion of the planter class to make merry with the Irish. A deep sectarian hatred-soaked atmosphere was encouraged by many anti-Catholic forces.

There was incredible historical prejudice against the Irish. In Virginia and Maryland, laws were passed to "prevent the importation of Papist priests."

As far back as 1696, anti-Irish Catholicism was rife. The Protestant clergy of Maryland wrote to the Bishop of London and complained that "large numbers of Irish papists are being brought annually into Maryland." Years later, in 1704, alarmed by the rising

Irish population, a bill was passed charging an import fee of "20 shillings" on all Irish Catholics imported into the province—these were undoubtedly indentured servants. There was a fine of five dollars for importing a Catholic secretly.

In 1728, the secretary of the Province of Pennsylvania expressed the fear that Irish Catholics "would overrun" the province. Another newspaper reported: "It is undoubtedly a fact the great numbers of Irish have of late years got into our colonies." With comments like that, the Catholics were clearly viewed as vermin taking over when they came in large numbers.

The issue of the numbers of Irish Catholics who fought for Washington is a vexed one. Major historians ignored or under-counted their numbers and, as very few Irish who arrived were literate, the assumption went unchallenged.

But clear evidence exists that there were far more Irish Catholics than the historical descriptions have allowed in the army of George Washington. Historian O'Brien originally counted ten thousand Irish names on the muster rolls and many more would have joined as the war progressed.

Like Lincoln two generations later, Washington warmly embraced those Irish who formed part of his circle.

In nearby Alexandria, Irish immigrant John Fitzgerald would play a major role in Washington's life. Washington's grandson, Park Custis, stated in his *Recollections* that Fitzgerald was Washington's "favorite aide" in the Revolution.

Washington mentions Fitzgerald eighty times in his diary; the first time was when he dined with the general at Mount Vernon on November 16, 1783.

Washington was also especially close to his neighbors, the McCarty family, who lived not far from Mount Vernon. Daniel McCarty and his family were one of only eleven families invited to Washington's funeral.

Washington's diaries contain no less than seventy-six references to time spent with different members of the McCarty family. There was clearly a great bond. Thaddeus McCarty's wedding took place at Washington's Mount Vernon residence, with Washington acting as witness.

It was common practice for the Washingtons to stop by the McCarty home every Sunday on their way home from church. Washington's papers at the Library of Congress record numerous business dealings covering land transactions between the two men.

Another friend was Irish native Oliver Pollock from Coleraine, County Derry and his wife Margaret O'Brien, a native of Clare. Pollock immigrated to the United States in 1760 and became a hugely successful businessman. He donated $300,000 (worth billions today) to the American army, and was credited with supplying most of the ammunition to the US Army. Not surprisingly, he became friendly with George Washington and the two men and their spouses dined together in Mount Vernon and other locations.

General George Rogers Clark, in 1785, told Congress he was only able to retain possession of Illinois with Pollock's financial help.

Washington also surrounded himself with Irish officers in his army and he enjoyed their *esprit de corps* and friendship. He especially liked to socialize with them on important occasions.

The Friendly Sons of Saint Patrick, a non-sectarian philanthropic organization founded in Philadelphia in March 1771—still a robust Irish organization today (women are now allowed)—was populated by leading Irish American figures from every professional background. Washington was a frequent guest.

An invitation to speak at a Friendly Sons gathering was very prestigious. As well as Washington, Thomas Jefferson and Alexander Hamilton both spoke at the organization's meetings.

While George Washington was not of Irish ancestry, he was unanimously adopted and was present to receive his honorary membership of the Friendly Sons on December 18, 1781.

They also presented him with a gold medal and attested it was being offered "with the warmest of hearts filled with the warmest attachments." Washington's signature on the attendance book is still clearly visible more than 220 years later. He stated: "I shall never cast my eyes on this badge but with grateful remembrance."

Washington became a regular attendee at their major events. On New Year's Eve, 1782, the Friendly Sons threw a dinner in his honor at James Byrnes's City Tavern in Philadelphia. We find him as late as 1787 attending the convention of the Friendly Sons. He clearly believed his own words that the Irish had a "firm adherence . . . to the glorious cause in which we are embarked."

We even find him offering a toast to the Irish at non-Irish events. On June 2, 1776 the *New-York Packet* reported Washington's attendance at the Provincial Congress held in New York.

The paper noted that thirty-one toasts were drunk. One toast the attendees, including Washington, drank to was: "May the generous Sons of Saint Patrick expel all the venomous reptiles of Britain."

So there was certainly no animosity. Quite the opposite, in fact: His view seemed to be colored by Ireland's own fight for freedom with which he seemed enamored. His sentiments were not just meant for the public space. Even in his private life, Washington had close Irish connections.

Away from the gilded halls, most Irish began life in America as indentured servants. Most were illiterate, so their voices were never heard at the time, or they were clearly viewed as vermin taking over when they came in large numbers.

Yet, like Lincoln two generations later, Washington warmly embraced those Irish who made it to America's shores. His relationship with the Irish in the army was excellent, and away from the battlefield, Washington was a willing guest and fiery speaker for the cause of Ireland at many Irish events.

Beyond the battlefield, it appeared Washington enjoyed the company of one Irishman almost more than any other friend.

Patrick O'Flynn was born in Ireland in 1748 and joined the Continental Army in Delaware. He made a new start after the war by opening a pub in the state.

His tavern was called "Sign of the Ship" and he was noted locally as an Irish wit, the kind of gregarious fellow that often ends up owning Irish pubs. He was also known as "The Captain."

Washington, it appears, dropped by very frequently as he was often passing through or doing business in the state.

Historian Michael O'Brien unearthed the obituary of O'Flynn when he died in July 1818.

Patrick O'Flynn, the obituary began, "kept a public house during the time that Congress sat in Philadelphia. It was always the stopping place for General Washington who generally remained a night and made a constant rule to meet the captain [on his visits]."

The obituary continues: "It was remarked on certain occasions by one of the gentlemen with Washington on those trips that in all his journeys with the president he had never seen him . . . with a man with whom he discoursed more familiar than with him [O'Flynn]. There were few men with whom Washington was as familiar. He was particularly said to enjoy the 'racy Irish wit of O'Flynn.'"

The image of Washington leaning over a bar listening to a saucy story or two helps humanize the man in a way. O'Flynn clearly accomplished what almost no other man could do, to pierce the legendary armor of discipline and self-fortitude of Washington and make him laugh.

Amazingly, the United Irishman leader, Theobald Wolfe Tone, often called the father of Irish nationhood, stopped off in the same pub a few years later. What a shame Washington was not there to sup with him.

So, despite efforts to write them out of history, whether it was fighting by his side; honoring his extraordinary prowess; rejoicing in his embrace of the cause of Ireland; or simply making him laugh, the Irish engendered a deep vein of trust, admiration, and understanding in George Washington. Those feelings of friendship, comity, and loyalty were clearly reciprocated.

CHAPTER 11

The Only Catholic to Sign the Declaration Was the Richest Man in America

C harles Carroll, born September 1737, the grandson of Irish immigrants from County Offaly, was the only Catholic signatory to the Declaration of Independence. At the time he dwelt in Maryland and was the richest man in America, worth in modern terms about $330 million.

He was the longest-living of all the signers of the declaration, ninety-five years old, when he passed away in November 1832.

His decision to back the Patriot side had massive implications. Throughout his life he accumulated huge political power through his wealth and contacts. When the seeds of revolution began to flourish, Carroll became an enormously important ally.

He did so because of his great anger at the foreign tax burden being placed on Americans by King George. Based in a strong anti-Catholic state in Maryland, his family wealth was all the more remarkable as a 1704 act had been passed "to prevent the growth of Popery in this Province," preventing Catholics from holding political office.

In 1768, he married his cousin, Mary "Molly" Darnall, and they had seven children, only three of whom lived. He later became both a state senator and a US senator after the 1704 act was no longer in effect.

He was also among the biggest slave owners in America by some accounts, owning more than a thousand human beings. He professed himself to be against slavery but never freed his own. Despite saying "Why keep alive the question of slavery? It is admitted by all to be a great evil," he did little to make that a reality. His bill in the Maryland legislature to gradually eliminate slavery was defeated.

He became president of the Maryland branch of the American Colonization Society organization aimed at sending African Americans back to Africa, but nothing came of it.

Carroll inherited his ten thousand acre estate and had a hand in a huge number of businesses, too many to list, but most notably the Baltimore Ohio railroad with other partners.

The Carrolls mixed with the cream of society, frequently entertaining George Washington and the Marquis de Lafayette. The massive house and grounds were the scenes for Maryland's major social events. Washington was a welcome visitor in good times and bad.

Washington also kept up a correspondence with him, urging him at one point to lead a peace delegation to meet with the Western Native Americans and praising his political and negotiating skills.

That letter written in January 1793 reads in part:

[As regards the commission] characters be appointed who are known to our citizens for their talents and integrity; and whose situation in life places them clear of every suspicion of a wish to prolong the war, or say rather whose interest, in common with that of their country, is clearly to produce peace . . . I have mentioned these difficulties to shew you, in the event of your declining, how serious they are, and to induce you to come forward and perform this important service to your country.

Carroll was the obvious leader of Maryland's drive for independence and was selected as delegate to the Continental Congress in

1776. He was part of a failed effort with Benjamin Franklin and Samuel Chase to induce French Canadians into the war on the side of the United States but the plan failed. He became best known for powerful articles written in the *Maryland Gazette* and signed by the pseudonym "First Citizen" which were very influential.

He was not present at the Continental Congress on July 4, 1776, so did not sign the historic document at the time. He did sign it a few months later—a brave step for a very wealthy man who knew his British opponents could make life very hard for him.

Influence ran deep in his family. His cousin, Archbishop John Carroll, penned the famous letter to Washington on behalf of Roman Catholics after the war, which strongly noted that the religious freedoms guaranteed in the federal Constitution were not yet granted by every state constitution.

Charles Carroll is also recalled in the third stanza of the state song "Maryland, My Maryland."

Thou wilt not cower in the dust,
Maryland! My Maryland!
Thy beaming sword shall never rust,
Maryland! My Maryland!
Remember Carroll's sacred trust,
Remember Howard's warlike thrust—
And all thy slumberers with the just,"

After the war, Washington paid tribute to the role Catholics played in the American Revolution:

As mankind becomes more liberal they will be more apt to allow that all those who conduct themselves as worthy members of the community are equally entitled to the protection of civil government. I hope ever to see America among the foremost nations in examples of justice and liberality. And I presume that your fellow-citizens will not forget the patriotic part which you took in the accomplishment of their

Revolution, and the establishment of their government; or the important assistance which they received from a nation in which the Roman Catholic faith is professed.

Archbishop John Carroll, the first Catholic bishop in the independent United States, and the brother of Daniel Carroll, a signer of the Constitution, and cousin of Charles Carroll, summed up Catholic participation in the Revolution:

> Their blood flowed as freely (in proportion to their numbers) to cement the fabric of independence as that of any of their fellow-citizens: They concurred with perhaps greater unanimity than any other body of men, in recommending and promoting that government, from whose influence America anticipates all the blessings of justice, peace, plenty, good order and civil and religious liberty.

The Founding Fathers

The Irish cabin boy who created the US Navy; the immigrant orphan who officially informed Washington he was president; the Irishman who witnessed Franklin's farewell to Washington; and Franklin's extraordinary letter from Ireland.

CHAPTER 12

By Land and By Sea—How a Former Irish Cabin Boy Founded the American Navy

On May 16, 1914, before a crowd of thousands on a balmy May afternoon in Washington's Franklin Square, President Woodrow Wilson unveiled a statue of John Barry, Irish-born founder of the American Navy and a Revolutionary War hero.

Every seat in the stands was filled, and thousands unable to gain admission stood in the streets or in nearby Franklin Park.

President Wilson said: "John Barry was an Irishman but his heart crossed the Atlantic with him . . . Commodore Barry . . . devoted an originating mind to the great cause which he intended to serve . . . This man illustrates for me all the splendid strength which we brought into this country by the magnet of freedom."

Congress had made fifty thousand dollars available for the construction of the statue and Congressman James Hamill did the honors on behalf of Congress.

Hamill was later an Irish American hero. He was the congressman from New Jersey who, in 1919, would demand that the US Congress receive Doctor Patrick McCartan as the ambassador from Ireland, thereby recognizing the nascent Irish Republic. (Congress refused.)

His tribute to Barry was short and eloquent: "First in our American pantheon stands the majestic figure of George Washington and close beside him John Barry on whose strong arms Washington was wont to lean with confidence in his hours of bitter anguish and trial: one the idolized father of our country, the other the venerated father of our navy."

Shortly after Harding's remarks, Miss Elisa Hepburn of Philadelphia, great-great-grandniece of Commodore Barry, was ushered into the speaker's box and pulled the rope that revealed the statue. The Marine Band played the national anthem and the newest monument in the Capitol was unveiled.

Another memorial to Irish-born Commandant John Barry, at the Naval Academy in Annapolis, Maryland, lays out his extraordinary achievement and place in history. It reads:

> February 22, 1797: At the Presidential Mansion in Philadelphia, President George Washington formally presented Irish-born John Barry with Commission Number One in the newly formed United States Navy. With the commission, backdated to the time of the original appointment, June 7, 1794, Washington formally reaffirmed his trust in Barry's leadership to establish the Navy under the Constitution.

The warm relationship between Washington and Barry was evident, as the following letter makes clear:

> To Captain John Barry
>   Head Quarters [Valley Forge], 12th March, 1778.
> Sir
> I have received your Letter of the 9th inst. and congratulate you upon the success which crowned your gallantry and address, in the late attack on the Enemy's Ships—altho circumstances prevented you from reaping the full benefit of your conquest, there is ample consolation in the degree of Glory which you have acquired—You will be pleased to accept of my sincere thanks, for the good things which you

have been so polite as to send me, with my wishes that suitable Success may always attend your Bravery. I am Sir Your most obedt Servt. George Washington.

The man who received all the accolades was a tenant farmer's son from a remote part of Ireland. John Barry grew up to become the founder of the American Navy and a hero of the revolution but he hardly started life with any expectation of such accomplishment.

John Barry was born in Ballysampson, a tiny village in County Wexford in Ireland, in 1739 or 1745, whichever version of history you believe. There appears to be evidence he disguised his age in order to qualify for major crew positions on ships he sailed on. He had a commanding presence, standing six foot three with the bearing and mien of a sea lord.

He was born to the sea. Wexford is one of Ireland's great ports. In nearby New Ross, the Famine Ships left a century or so later. Among those seeking a new life at that time was Patrick Kennedy, great-grandfather of JFK.

In Bannow Bay, another Wexford port, the English lord Strongbow arrived in 1169 at the invitation of the displaced king of Leinster, Diarmuid Mac Murchada. His name resounds in Irish history, much like that of Benedict Arnold does in the United States. From that invitation began an Anglo Norman invasion that lasts in parts of Ireland to this very day.

Barry grew up Catholic on a tenant farmer's piteous holding, but was drawn to the ocean like lightning to a storm. From an early age, an uncle tutored him in the ways of the sea and young Barry proved a quick learner.

With no local employment and the Penal Laws blocking education, he became a cabin boy on a merchant ship at the age of nine. As mentioned, there's quite a good chance he may have presented himself as older than he actually was to get the position.

Once on board, Barry was a natural sailor, needing no extensive landlubber training but picking up the essentials himself. He felt he was born for the sea, he told friends in later life.

Around 1762, Barry departed Irish shores for good, working as the second mate on a vessel that sailed to Philadelphia Harbor. The American Revolution was still far off, but Barry brought with him a tenacious hatred of the British and their occupation of Ireland. From the start, he was implacably opposed to their presence in America.

Once landed in the new world, his nautical skills saw him become a major figure on the Philadelphia docks. His social skills ensured his access later into Philadelphia society, where the tall and dashing young Irish sea captain had many admirers.

He would marry Mary Cleary in 1768, but she passed away. He married again in 1777 to Sarah Austin. Though they had no children of their own, they raised the two sons of his sister and brother-in-law, both of whom died young.

As for his nautical career, in 1766 we know he was captain of the ship called *Barbados* which departed Philadelphia for that island. The ship had once been used by slave traders, but carried legitimate cargo when Barry sailed it.

By the time the Revolution was stirring, Barry was a highly-regarded seaman and a dominant figure in Philadelphia nautical circles. We know he sailed from Britain to Philadelphia as captain of the *Black Prince* in mid-October 1775.

By the time he returned in 1776, all had changed. Revolution was in the air and the Second Continental Congress had met, with the need to establish an American fleet among the priorities. The complete dominance of the British navy on the high seas was well known and the Americans had to respond.

The infant navy faced a massively daunting task. The British navy was the most skilled in the world. One hundred and sixty ships would later sail in from Canadian waters in an English armada to capture New York. Washington and his men did not have as much as a rowboat.

Washington wanted American warships on the high seas to harass and harry the British man of war ships. His quartermaster, Stephen Moylan from Cork, was tasked with making ships ready and Barry, who was a close friend of Moylan, was the ideal man to command a ship for service.

The great sailing tradition along the East Coast of America meant there were able-bodied mariners ready to go to war against the British fleet. The problem was outfitting boats and training men.

Two ships were purchased, the *Lexington* and the *Reprisal*, and John Barry was commissioned as captain of the *Lexington*. He was the first Catholic, incidentally, appointed to any major position by the Continental Congress.

On November 23, 1775, the US Navy came into being. The *Lexington* was the first ship to achieve widespread fame. The name of John Barry and his exploits were soon on many lips.

The British were sailing in convoys. They had the ocean to themselves until Barry—on board his newly-fitted ship, the *Lexington*—encountered the British warship *Edward* on April 7, 1776. After battling for an hour, the *Edward* hauled down her Union Jack and surrendered. It was the first surrender of a British ship to the newly-created American Navy.

Barry's report to General Washington runs thus: "I have the pleasure to acquaint you that at one pm this day I fell in with the sloop *Edward* . . . She engaged us and they killed two of our men and wounded two more. We shattered her in a terrible manner. I shall give you soon an account of the powder and arms taken from her."

Captain Henry Bellew, the British commander of the *Edward*, wrote an abject letter of apology to Admiral Molineux Shuldham, his commander in chief in London, after the *Edward* surrender. The letter is dated June 10, 1776: "I believe Captain Hamond informed you of my very great misfortune, in having been taken by the rebel privateer."

The sight of the captured *Edward*, her flag hauled down, sailing into Philadelphia, excited the colonists like little else. The capture became a focus in Congress, where funding for the navy suddenly became a hot topic.

Barry became known to the British as a terror on the high seas. Try as they might, they could never run down the *Lexington* with its masterful captain on board. At one time, four British ships set off in pursuit but Barry evaded them all.

Barry's biographer, Joseph Gurn, author of *Commander John Barry, Father of the American Navy*, wrote: "The little brig *Lexington* mocking the might of the British navy must have been a severe strain on the enemy pride."

Most importantly with the French fleet engaging, parity on the high seas would become a reality. Barry's exploits were music to the ears of Washington and the nautical hero communicated directly with the general to keep him abreast of his naval victories:

> Port Penn [Delaware River] On March 9th 1778
> Dear General
> Tis with the Greatest Satisfaction Imaginable I inform You of Capturing two Ships & a Schooner of the Enemy. The two Ships were Transports from Rhode Island Loaded with forage One Mounting Six four Pounders with fourteen hands Each the Schooner is in the Engineering Department Mounting Eight Double fortified four Pounders & twelve four Pound howitz Properly fitted in Every Particular & Manned with thirty three men.

Barry was the most feared enemy that the British navy faced. The sight of his ship on the horizon was enough to cause the vapors among the British seamen.

John Barry Kelly, writing on USHistory.org, captures Barry's success with clarity and precision:

> In the space of 58 years, this son of a poor Irish farmer rose from humble cabin boy to senior commander of the entire United States fleet. Intrepid In battle, he was humane to his men as well as adversaries and prisoners.
> Barry's war contributions are unparalleled: he was the first to capture a British war vessel on the high seas; he captured two British ships after being severely wounded in a

ferocious sea battle; he quelled three mutinies; he fought on land at the Battles of Trenton and Princeton; he captured over 20 ships including an armed British schooner in the lower Delaware; he authored a Signal Book which established a set of signals used for effective communication between ships; and he fought the last naval battle of the American Revolution aboard the frigate *Alliance* in 1783.

Barry was all-in on his fight against the hated British, whose penal laws had deeply impacted his impoverished family back home.

Barry would fight by land and by sea. When his ship the *Effingham* was not ready and needed extensive repairs, Barry volunteered to join the Continental Army on land in order to fight on.

Admiral George Henry Preble, a navy officer and historian, recounted that Barry "took part in the battles of Princeton and Trenton, two of the most important battles of the war." Preble added: "His dashing bravery and cool judgement won the admiration of all . . . In the winter of 1776 he served with distinction and obtained the command of a company of volunteers and with some heavy cannon."

Once back in the ocean, Barry was becoming such a pivotal figure that the British general Lord Howe attempted to turn him into a nautical Benedict Arnold. Unsuccessfully, as it turned out—Barry stated that he "spurned the idea of being a traitor."

A glimpse of Barry's brilliance at sea is given by Benjamin Franklin in a note written in November 1781 dealing with foreign treatment of American prisoners:

The Ambassador of Venice told me that he was charged by the Senate to express to me their grateful Sense of the Friendly Behavior of Capt Barry, Commander of the Alliance, in rescuing one of the Ships of their State from an English Privateer, and setting her at Liberty. And he requested me to communicate this Acknowledgement to Congress.

During the war, Barry commanded the following ships (the *Effingham* had been destroyed before she was fully completed to avoid use by the British): the *Delaware*, the *Lexington*, the *Raleigh*, the *Alliance*, and the *United States*.

The Irish have not forgotten him. The Ancient Order of Hibernians, America's largest Irish group, holds an Admiral Barry Day every September 13. They have also fought for more recognition of Barry.

His was an extraordinary life and career; his deeds eulogized almost a century and a half later by US President Woodrow Wilson. It was a fitting tribute to the man who came by sea from a small land far away and who would help to save the American Revolution.

CHAPTER 13

The Irish Orphan Who Became a Founding Father and Informed Washington He Was Elected President

If there is a more unlikely success story than that of Irish emigrant Charles Thomson in Revolutionary-era America, it has yet to be told. From homeless orphan to Founding Father, to secretary of the Continental Congress (essentially the speaker), the Maghera, Derry native defied his homeless history to be the man chosen to proudly and personally inform George Washington that he had been elected president.

No Irish-born person in America has achieved the stature and rank he did. He is on the back of the two dollar bill, standing beside John Hancock as he signs the Declaration of Independence. He created the Great Seal of the United States which is so familiar to us today on every important federal document; he was the first to inform Washington of his election as president; and he was among the leaders in Philadelphia of the resistance to the British Army.

As secretary of the Continental Congress, he kept every record of every major speech with meticulous accuracy so future generations would be able to access the all-important archive.

He was a confidant of Washington, Jefferson, and especially Franklin and decried slavery to all of them.

Originally, he was one of only two signatories to the Declaration of Independence, the other being printer and fellow Ulster Irishman John Dunlop. The rest of the signatures came later.

No Irish person was regarded as highly by George Washington, a fact the commander-in-chief made clear.

Thomson was a fierce American nationalist who trumpeted the need to go to war with the despised British. Unlike most of the Founding Fathers, he despised slavery. He paid his farmworkers the going rate, even dividing some of that land for them so they could build homes.

He argued with Jefferson and told him slavery was like a cancer on the new country.

Incredibly, he is mostly a forgotten figure, though often designated as one of the Founding Fathers, which assuredly he was.

Anonymity became inevitable when he destroyed his magnum opus, his inside account of the insurrection and the events leading up to and away from it. He had allegedly written a thousand-page diary which was apparently unflattering to many of the great names. But he burned it.

He knew the realities of how the great men of the time were filled with jealousy, greed, and ambition along with their renowned qualities.

Doctor Benjamin Rush, who signed the Declaration of Independence, rated Thomson "a man of great learning and general knowledge. He was an intimate friend of John Dickinson the man who helped lead the original protest against the Stamp Act."

Once in Rush's company, Thomson explained his reluctance to publish his memoir:

> No . . . I ought not, for I should contradict all the histories of the great events of the revolution, and show by my account of men, motives and measures, that we are wholly indebted to . . . Providence for its successful issue.
>
> Let the world admire the supposed wisdom and valor of our great men. Perhaps they may adopt the qualities that

have been ascribed to them and thus good may be done. I shall not undeceive future generations.

Selflessly, he decided the battle had been won—there was no good reason to besmirch or deride the reputations of those who had created the almost magical new country against all odds and it would be a grave mistake to do it.

By so doing he knew he was downplaying his own role in history, but he decided it was better to let the narrative be written without his input.

Besides, he was not a bitter man. How could he be with his rags to riches story?

His own rise to prominence would outstrip even the most unbelievable fable of success of a man against overwhelming odds.

In his own life, Thomson had every right to fail, to be unable to overcome his tragic childhood, but instead he persevered, never letting life's limitations or class differences stop him.

Life threw a knockout punch right from the start. His mother died when he was very young, leaving his father with six children to raise.

Looking around the impoverished rural Derry countryside, John Thomson felt his family's only chance lay in America. Many hard-working Presbyterians and many dissenters, both Catholic and Protestant, were repressed and under the heel of the British. No viable future beckoned for a widower with six young children except, perhaps, the workhouse.

The only solution was the New World. Many in Thomson's circle had departed for what the Irish called in their mother tongue: "The Fresh Land."

Thus, Charles, then ten years old in 1739, left for America from his native townland of Maghera in County Derry with his father and five siblings. His father hoped to start life afresh in the new country, but he unfortunately never set foot in it.

Within sight of land, he succumbed to ship fever, leaving the children orphaned. Charles closed his father's eyes for the last time.

He remembered the moment: "I stood by the bed-side of my expiring and much loved father, closed his eyes and performed my last filial duty on him."

Worse was to come; the unscrupulous captain stole their father's possessions and landed the six orphans on the quayside in Delaware Bay where the ship had landed. They were penniless with no one to meet them and nowhere to go.

It certainly was a most unpromising start in life.

Yet, the same person who sat on the quayside alone on February 5, 1739 would singlehandedly represent the new original states of the United States and ride from New York to Washington's home of Mount Vernon to personally inform the new leader that he had been chosen unanimously by voters as America's first president.

By then, Charles Thomson had become secretary of the Continental Congress, essentially taking the position of house speaker and aspects of the secretary of state of the first ever lasting democratic institution set up anywhere in the world.

The man who rode out to inform Washington, once a lonely little boy at the harbor, was now a giant in American history.

He was a mathematics whiz; an accomplished scholar of Greek who would translate the bible from Greek to English; and a fearless fighter for justice, even when it came to the Native American tribes around Pennsylvania who had given him the honorific "he who speaks the truth."

His name kindled immediate respect. On August 30, 1774, John Adams stated in his diary: "We had much Conversation with Mr. Charles Thomson. This Charles Thomson is Sam Adams of Philadelphia—the Life of the Cause of Liberty."

How did he come to embody so much respect and trust even to the point of becoming recognized as a Founding Father?

After landing on the quayside, Thomson was taken in by a local blacksmith who saved him from destitution but also likely indentured him.

Soon, he tired of the work, and in possession of a bright mind and endless ambition to better himself he ascertained from a female friend where the best school in the area was. He made his way to the school and, for the first time in his brief life, caught a break.

The principal, Francis Alison, was a Donegal native and immediately saw a boy with massive potential and even arranged for him to live with his family.

Thus, he was admitted to Francis Alison's school in New London, Pennsylvania. There he became a top class scholar of Greek and Latin and eventually a teacher.

Within a few years, he would make the acquaintance of Benjamin Franklin and become one of his close associates. He would also become a tutor himself at the Philadelphia Academy, which would eventually evolve into the University of Pennsylvania.

As the distant drums of war beckoned, Thomson became a committed Patriot, mindful of his own family's persecution in Ireland and the landless Irish people's battle against the British.

His work among the Native Americans and his insistence they be treated correctly added greatly to his reputation as a fair-minded man.

His friendship with Ben Franklin, who saw a kindred soul in the young Irishman, was also of vital importance.

He was against the British in North America even before the Revolutionary War started. When Parliament passed the Stamp Act in 1765, Franklin sent a letter to Thomson from London that "the sun of liberty is set, and Americans must light the lamps of industry and economy."

Thomson replied: "Be assured that we shall light torches of a very different sort."

As the battle for freedom loomed, Thomson was first on board. By now he was a prosperous merchant and a senior figure in the Patriot ranks in Philadelphia.

A superb diarist and observer, he became the obvious choice for secretary to the Continental Congress—the defiant young parliament created by the Revolutionaries. It was a position far more exalted than the title might suggest. He would stay in that key position throughout the war, eventually clocking up fifteen years.

As the secretary, he recorded every vote and every discussion and he was known to be impartial and fair. Under the new dispensation, when the war was won and Washington was elected president, Thomson, as the most powerful official in the congress, was deputed to inform President-Elect Washington of his success and election as president. It would be no easy task, as he would discover.

As Ron Chernow noted in his book *Washington: A Life*:

> The legislators had chosen a fine emissary. A well-rounded man, known for his work in astronomy and mathematics, the Irish-born Thomson . . . rejoiced that the new president would be Washington, whom he venerated as someone singled out by Providence to be "the savior and father" of the country. Having known Thomson since the Continental Congress, Washington esteemed him as a faithful public servant and exemplary patriot.

It was not easy getting to Mount Vernon. In fact, it was an exhausting ride. Thomson recalled a horseback journey to Virginia, which was "much impeded by tempestuous weather, bad roads, and the many large rivers I had to cross."

In fact, the formal handing over of power had to be delayed from March to April because of spring river swells and the near impassable condition of many roads.

Thomson finally reached his destination and was met by Washington. Both men were very formal as the occasion dictated. A contemporary painting showed Washington, legs crossed, sitting at his bureau, his chair swung around to listen to Thomson (He actually had one of the first ever swivel chairs, given to him by the French) as he declared that the United States had come into being. Washington had won the election for first president held February 4 by sixty-nine votes to zero in the Electoral College, a unanimous verdict. John Adams would be his vice president.

Thomson stated: "I am honored with the commands of the Senate to wait upon your Excellency with the information of your being elected to the office of President of the United States of America by a unanimous vote. This commission was entrusted to me on account of my having been long in the Confidence of the late Congress."

There was no certainty Washington would accept. Like Cincinnatus, he had returned home gladly after the fight was won. Washington was serene and comfortable in his beloved Virginia.

In letters to friends he cited the "ocean of difficulties" he faced and added he was relinquishing "all expectations of private happiness" in the world. He was also fifty-seven, a good age for the times, and feared the clock would run out before the presidential term was served. He loved Virginia and Mount Vernon was his castle, but Thomson's arrival forced him to a decision.

Thus Thomson was much relieved when Washington, with many caveats as per his usual careful way, accepted the position of first president of the United States.

It was a glorious moment for the Derryman to share, the confirmation that Washington would be president. One wonders if he cast his mind back to that young orphan boy arriving on a friendless shore and pondered the incredible journey he had undertaken so successfully.

Washington continued: "While I realize the arduous nature of the task which is conferred on me and feel my inability to perform it, I wish there may not be reason for regretting the choice. All I can promise is only that which can be accomplished by an honest zeal."

Washington knew he had to be en route as soon as possible and asked Thomson to accompany him. He paid his old comrade a special tribute:

Upon considering how long a time some of the Gentlemen of both Houses of Congress have been at New York, how anxiously desirous they must be to proceed to business, and how deeply the public mind appears to be impressed with the necessity of doing it speedily, I can not find myself at liberty to delay my journey. I shall therefore be in readiness to set out the day after tomorrow and shall be happy in the pleasure of your company; for you will permit me to say that it is a peculiar gratification to have received the communication from you.

Thus it was that the president and the former pauper set course for New York in Washington's stately carriage. Also on board was David Humphreys, Washington's aide.

Washington came close to a rare show of private emotion as he recalled the moment of his departure from home:

About ten o'clock I bade adieu to Mount Vernon, to private life, and to domestic felicity; and with a mind oppressed with more anxious and painful sensations than I have words to express, set out for New York in company with Mr. Charles Thomson, and Colonel Humphries, with the best dispositions to render service to my country in obedience to its call, but with less hope of answering its expectations.

On the triumphal journey, Thomson witnessed the incredible scenes as hundreds of thousands turned out to cheer Washington on his way. This culminated in a spectacular arrival into New York City where a massive welcome parade took place and streets were thronged with revelers as the new president completed his inauguration.

On his retirement in 1789, Thomson wrote to Washington, remembering those extraordinary times:

Sir,
Having had the honor of serving in quality of Secretary of Congress from the first meeting of Congress in 1774 to the present time, a period of almost fifteen years, and having seen in that eventful period, by the interposition of divine Providence the rights of our country asserted and vindicated, its independence declared acknowledged and fixed, peace & tranquility restored & in consequence thereof a rapid advance in arts, manufacturing and population, and lastly

a government established which gives well grounded hopes of promoting its lasting welfare & securing its freedom and happiness, I now wish to return to private life.

With this intent I present myself before you to surrender up the charge of the books, records and papers of the late Congress which are in my custody & deposited in rooms of the house where the legislature assemble, and to deliver into your hands the Great Seal of the federal Union, the keeping of which was one of the duties of my Office, and the seal of the Admiralty which was committed to my care when that board was dissolved.

Even though Thomson was not given a position in the new federal government, Washington clearly respected his service to his country. In his July 24, 1789, letter to Thomson, Washington wrote:

I have to regret that the period of my coming again into public life, should be exactly that, in which you are about to retire from it. The present age does so much justice to the unsullied reputation with which you have always conducted yourself in the execution of the duties of your Office, and Posterity will find your Name so honorably connected with the verification of such a multitude of astonishing facts, that my single suffrage would add little to the illustration of your merits. Yet I cannot withhold any just testimonial, in favor of a so old, so faithful and so able public officer, which might tend to sooth his mind in the shade of retirement. Accept, then, this serious Declaration, that your Services have been important, as your patriotism was distinguished; and enjoy that best of all rewards, the consciousness of having done your duty well.

Thomson replied: "I cannot find words to express the feelings of my heart, on the receipt of your favour of yesterday, at this repeated instance of your goodness."

Thomson lived to the age of ninety-three, dying in 1828. His sense of honor, decency, and empathy for the common man was never more evident than when he explained the meaning of the Great Seal he had chosen. At its heart, he explained, it was about peace, and not war.

Here is what he said:

The Escutcheon is composed of the chief & pale, the two most honorable ordinaries. The Pieces, paly, represent the several states all joined in one solid compact entire, supporting a Chief, which unites the whole & represents Congress. The Motto alludes to this union. The pales in the arms are kept closely united by the chief and the Chief depends upon that union & the strength resulting from it for its support, to denote the Confederacy of the United States of America & the preservation of their union through Congress.

The colours of the pales are those used in the flag of the United States of America; White signifies purity and innocence, Red, hardiness & valor, and Blue, the colour of the Chief signifies vigilance, perseverance & justice. The Olive branch and arrows denote the power of peace & war which is exclusively vested in Congress. The Constellation denotes a new State taking its place and rank among other sovereign powers. The Escutcheon is born on the breast of an American Eagle without any other supporters to denote that the United States of America ought to rely on their own Virtue.

The motto, of course, is "E Pluribus Unum" (Out of Many One), a line chosen by Thomson to convey the union of hearts and minds in pursuit of a common goal. He exemplified that sentiment in his own life. Sadly, there are no monuments to Charles Thomson in America or Ireland today, a gross oversight considering his extraordinary role in creating American freedom.

CHAPTER 14

The Remarkable Irishman Who Witnessed Washington and Franklin's Last Meeting—and Corrected Washington's Writings

Irish-born Robert Carr will never be among the illustrious names of leaders of the American Revolution, but he witnessed more history as Ben Franklin's aide and errand boy than most will see in several lifetimes.

Back in 1861, the then eighty-three-year-old Carr gave his final interview to oral historian Benson John Lossing. His mental faculties were in fine order, and he looked at the past with a gimlet eye. Times, people, places, faces—he remembered them all with exactitude, said his interviewer.

Lossing described him as of "stout build, [a] vigorous man possessed of sound health and remarkable buoyancy of spirits." He told the historian he had not been sick in more than sixty years.

He lived with Ben Franklin in the latter months of Franklin's life, and he discussed with Lossing the poignant moment he witnessed when, in April 1789, Washington, on his way to assume the office of president, stopped by to see his old friend, by then battling a number of maladies, for the last time.

It was truly a meeting of magnificent minds. It is doubtful if there was ever a more significant coming together than that of the military genius who won the war that changed the world and the man who won the diplomatic victory—bringing the French in, negotiating the Treaty of Paris, and playing a leading role in the creation of the vital core documents that shaped the new Republic.

As the George Washington Mount Vernon historical record noted: "George Washington may rightly be known as the 'Father of his Country' but, for the two decades before the American Revolution, Benjamin Franklin was the world's most famous American."

Franklin was more than a political genius; his experiments with electricity won him the Copley Medal—the eighteenth century equivalent of the Nobel Prize. It was just one of many inventions Franklin created that set him apart as a great scientist.

He was also deeply political. Due in part to his experience of living in Britain for eighteen months, where he encountered a deep strain of anti-Americanism, he became a fierce American patriot, even breaking with his own son, who remained a Tory and who was cut out of his father's will as punishment.

He was also radicalized by Ireland, and remarked: "All Ireland is strongly in favour of the American cause. They have reason to sympathise with us."

Benjamin Franklin toured Ireland in 1771 and was deeply impacted by the astounding level of poverty he found there.

It was a trip of great revelation to him, as he saw the consequences of what happened when a country was ground down under an imperial master's boot. He saw Ireland for what it was: a fully-owned and deeply neglected pariah province of Great Britain.

He wrote to a friend:

The people in that unhappy country are in a most wretched situation. Ireland is itself a poor country, and Dublin a magnificent city; but the appearances of general extreme poverty among the lower people are amazing. They live in wretched hovels of mud and straw, are clothed in rags, and subsist chiefly on potatoes. Our New England farmers, of the poorest sort, in regard to the enjoyment of all the comforts of life, are princes when compared to them. Perhaps three-fourths of the Inhabitants are in this situation.

In 1977, the US government presented a commemorative bust of Franklin to mark the visit. Speaking at the unveiling of the bust, then Ambassador Walter J. P. Curley noted that:

Franklin's friendship for Ireland was no fleeting whim. He had said, "You have ever been friendly to the rights of mankind and we acknowledge with pleasure and gratitude that your nation has produced patriots who have nobly distinguished themselves in the cause of humanity and America."

Franklin had his Irish experience in mind, no doubt, when he was one of the committee of five appointed to draft the Declaration of Independence. He was the only man to sign the three key documents in the birth of the United States: the Declaration of Independence, the Treaty of Paris, and the Constitution.

As the Mount Vernon historical journal states:

As the United States' minister in France from 1776, Franklin brought the French into the war against Britain and kept them there. This made him second only to Washington for his importance in winning the War of American Independence.

Together with George Washington, he acted as a senior statesman willing to lend his authority to the compromises they deemed necessary to forge a Constitution capable of serving the new nation.

There was one important difference between the two men—Franklin strongly rejected his early acceptance of slavery and sent anti-slavery petitions to Congress while Washington prevaricated on the issue.

In the final letters between Washington and Franklin, their love and regard for each other is noted—a "great affection was added to the two men's customary mutual respect and admiration," as one contemporary of the two men wrote.

The final correspondence between the two men clearly shows that. Franklin died on April 17, 1790. Here are just two examples of that love and respect:

To George Washington from Benjamin Franklin, September, 16 1789

Philada Sept. 16. 1789

Dear Sir,

My Malady renders my Sitting up to write rather painful to me, but I cannot let my Son-in-law Mr Bache part for New York, without congratulating you by him on the Recovery of your Health, so precious to us all, and on the growing Strength of our New Government under your Administration.

For my own personal Ease, I should have died two Years ago; but tho' those Years have been spent in excruciating Pain, I am pleas'd that I have liv'd them, since they have brought me to see our present Situation. I am now finishing my 84th and probably with it my Career in this Life; but in whatever State of Existence I am plac'd hereafter, if I retain any Memory of what has pass'd here, I shall with it retain the Esteem, Respect, and Affection with which I have long been, my dear Friend, Yours most sincerely

To Benjamin Franklin from George Washington

New York Septr 23d 1789.

Dear Sir,

The affectionate congratulations on the recovery of my health—and the warm expressions of personal friendship which were contained in your favor of the 16th inst. claim my gratitude. And the consideration that it was written when you were afflicted with a painful malady, greatly increases my obligation for it.

Would to God, my dear Sir, that I could congratulate you upon the removal of that excruciating pain under which you labour! and that your existence might close with as much ease to yourself, as its continuance has been beneficial to our Country & useful to Mankind—or, if the united wishes of a free people, joined with the earnest prayers of every friend to science & humanity could relieve the body from pains or infirmities, you could claim an exemption on this score. But this cannot be, and you have within yourself the only resource to which we can confidently apply for relief—a philosophic mind.

If to be venerated for benevolence—if to be admired for talent—if to be esteemed for patriotism—if to be beloved for philanthropy can gratify the human mind, you must have the pleasing consolation to know that you have not lived in vain; and I flatter my self that it will not be ranked among the least grateful occurrences of your life to be assured that so long as I retain my memory—you will be thought on with respect, veneration and affection by Dear Sir Your sincere friend and obedient Hble Servant

Go: Washington

So these were the two giants of men who embraced on April 29, 1789, for the last time, as Robert Carr looked on as a witness. It was a historic moment.

Carr's contact with Washington did not end there, however. He also recalled acting as Washington's proofreader for articles the president wanted to be published in an influential newspaper at that time owned by Franklin's grandson. Later, under the influence of Thomas Jefferson, the same publication would become viciously partisan against him.

At the time of the interview, Carr was one of the few surviving Americans who knew Washington and Franklin personally. As to his advancing age, he stated: "I try to forget the miseries which were few and to remember the mercies which were great."

Carr came from Ireland to Pennsylvania when he was just six years old but retained a strong Irish accent all his life. His father was a schoolteacher in Philadelphia and, by sheer coincidence, they lived next door to Franklin.

Ben Franklin was a rare genius and a man who would have shattered the Mensa scales if Mensa had been around back then.

Remembering his time with this remarkable Founding Father, Carr stated:

> We lived next door to Doctor Franklin in Market Street and he seemed to think much of my father who was frequently in his house by invitation . . . I sometimes went there with my father and Franklin treated me very kindly, always having a pleasant word for me.
>
> I was about ten years old when Franklin asked my father to allow me to do errands for him. Young as I was, he sent me everywhere to the butcher, the grocer, the printers, the book-stores the doctor and to certain gentlemen in the city.

Carr recalled that "[Franklin] was sick most of the time while I was with him, often suffering great pain with his malady [he suffered from gout and pleurisy] and yet he continued to write a great deal. I think he wrote two or three pamphlets during the last year of his life. I carried his manuscripts to the printers and also the proof sheets [Franklin's grandson, Benjamin Franklin Bache, trained Carr in the printing trade]."

Robert Carr actually lived with Franklin for the last few months of his life: "For three months before he died I was in his room a great deal to do errands for the doctors, his attendant and for the family. For two or three weeks I remember Doctor Jones [an eminent local physician] came several times every day and brought Doctor Rush with him."

Franklin was taking opium for the pain, as recommended by his doctor, who also took care of President Washington. Despite its blunting impact on his mental capacities, his brain remained sharp, according to Carr.

Carr witnessed the dying Franklin meeting George Washington for the last time, in Franklin's house.

Said Carr: "I remember when Washington called to see him while on his way to New York to be inaugurated President of the United States. They embraced like brothers. Franklin had been suffering much pain that morning but was relieved at the time of the president's call when his manner was cheerful, almost playful at times for he was rejoiced to see his friend. They never met again on this earth."

Carr went on to describe his relationship with Washington himself.

Carr had proven himself an expert proofreader and Franklin's grandson, Benjamin Franklin Bache, had started a newspaper called *The Advertiser* and employed him regularly.

The seat of government had moved to Philadelphia at this point and Washington was very friendly with young Bache because of the Franklin connection and often wrote articles for his publication.

It fell to Carr to proofread and edit the articles.

"I carried corrected proof-sheets to President Washington and sometimes assisted him in the reading and making proper printer's marks for corrections which he did not always understand," he said.

However, Washington's friendship with Bache soon cooled as Thomas Jefferson took over the paper and began making scandalous attacks on Washington and members of his cabinet. Jefferson wanted war with England; Washington urged great caution.

While we may think today our politics are suffused with hatred and dispute, it is worth recalling that politics was a vicious sport back then too, as the following extract demonstrates.

The Jefferson-inspired editorial attack on Washington ran:

If ever a nation was debauched by a man the American nation has been debauched by Washington. Let his conduct then be an example for future ages, let it serve to be a warning that no man may be an idol. Let the history of the Federal Government instruct mankind that the mask of patriotism may be worn to conceal the foulest designs against the liberties of the people.

Carr remembered the alarm when the newspaper, now called *The Aurora,* launched an especially vitriolic attack on Washington:

I distinctly remember the great excitement in Philadelphia caused by an outrageous article against Washington, a day or two after he retired from the presidency. I well remember that butchers of Spring Garden, who had been soldiers under Washington, were so incensed that they marched in a body to attack *The Aurora* offices. They threw its types into the streets and nearly destroyed the inside of the room. Publisher Bache was personally assaulted on the street.

Renowned for his proofreading ability, Carr was hired by Irish-born Charles Thomson, permanent secretary of the Continental Congress, who was translating the Old Testament from the original Greek into English.

As for Franklin, when asked to describe him physically, Carr stated:

When I knew him he was a strong-built man over 80-years of age about five foot nine inches in stature and inclined to corruption [stooping].

His complexion was fair though he was an old man, his eyes were gray and very bright when engaged in conversation . . . Franklin was polite and kind to everyone whether he was a servant or a senator, for he was always a gentleman.

Thus did an Irish immigrant remember his encounters with two of the greatest men in American history, humanizing them both for us in a way that no historian can.

Robert Carr would go on to become a colonel in a Pennsylvania regiment and fight with honor during the War of 1812. Subsequently, he and his wife ran Philadelphia Botanical Gardens and he was elected as an alderman and later Justice of the Peace.

He had a sad latter part of his life; his businesses failed and he was forced to live in a room lent by a friend who was governor of the insane asylum. His witness to history was an invaluable contribution to understanding the tenor of the times and the final farewell between two of the greatest American heroes.

CHAPTER 15

Extract from Benjamin Franklin's Remarkable Letter from Ireland

Ben Franklin's prophetic letter from Ireland to Thomas Cushing, the Boston merchant and widely respected politician, is worth quoting substantially when it comes to his observations about the Irish situation. (Much else about the New England political situation is not relevant and has been omitted.)

At a party in late 1771, hosted by George Townshend, the lord lieutenant of Ireland in Dublin, Franklin suddenly encounters his arch foe, Lord Hillsborough, the secretary of state for the Colonies. The two have been at loggerheads over the issue of self-rule for the colonies. (Hillsborough was an avowed hardliner on retaining the colonies.) The encounter and aftermath is described in fine detail by Franklin.

There is also in the letter, the unbridled joy of Franklin at being so warmly received by the Irish parliament and his observation about Ireland and America having a common enemy. His conclusion that both countries could join forces against Britain is a strong indication of the tenor of the times and the pro-American sentiment very prevalent in Ireland.

To Thomas Cushing

London, Jany. 13. 1772

Sir,

I am now return'd again to London from a Journey of some Months in Ireland and Scotland ... As there is something curious in our Interview [his encounter with Lord Hillsborough] in Ireland, I must give you an Account of it. I met with him accidentally at the Lord Lieutenant's, who happened to invite us to dine, with a large Company, on the same Day. He was surprizingly civil, and urg'd my Fellow-travelersl and me to call at his House in our intended Journey Northwards, where we might be sure of better Accommodations than the Inns could afford us. He press'd us so politely that it was not easy to refuse without apparent Rudeness, as we must pass through his Town of Hillsborough and by his Door; and as it might afford an Opportunity of saying something on American Affairs, I concluded to comply with his Invitation.

His Lordship went home some time before we left Dublin; we call'd upon him, and were detain'd at his House four Days, during which time he entertain'd us with great Civility, and a particular Attention to me that appear'd the more extraordinary as I knew that but just before I left London he had express'd himself concerning me in very angry Terms, calling me a Republican, a factious mischievous Fellow, and the like.

In our Conversations he first show'd himself a good Irishman, [Although born in England, Hillsborough held an Irish title] blaming England for its Narrowness towards that Country, in restraining its Commerce, discouraging its Woollen Manufactury, &c. and when I apply'd his Observations to America, he said he had always been of Opinion that the People in every Part of the King's Dominions had a natural Right to make the best Use they could of the Productions of their Country: and that America ought not to be restrain'd in manufacturing any thing she could manufacture to Advantage; that he suppos'd she at present found generally more Profit in Agriculture; but whenever she found that less profitable, or a particular Manufacture more so, he had no objection to her persuing it; and he censur'd Lord Chatham for asserting in his Speech that the Parliament had a Right or ought to restrain Manufactures in the Colonies.

He seem'd attentive to every thing that might make my Stay in his House agreable to me, and put his eldest Son, Lord Kilwarling, into his Phaeton [Carriage] with me to drive me a Round of Forty Miles, that I might see the Country, the Seats, Manufactures, &c. covering me with his own Cloak lest I should take Cold: and, in short, seem'd in every thing extreamly solicitous to impress me, and the Colonies through me, with a good Opinion of him:

All which I could not but wonder at, knowing that he likes neither them nor me; and I thought it inexplicable but on the Supposition that he apprehended an approaching Storm, and was desirous of lessening beforehand the Number of Enemies he had so imprudently created. . .

. . . Before I leave Ireland I must mention that being desirous of seeing the principal Patriots there, I staid till the Opening of their Parliament. I found them dispos'd to be Friends of America, in which Disposition I endeavoured to confirm them, with the Expectation that our growing Weight might in time be thrown into their Scale, and, by joining our Interest with theirs, might be obtained for them as well as for us, a more equitable Treatment from this Nation. There are many brave Spirits among them, the Gentry are a very sensible, polite and friendly People. Their Parliament makes a most respectable Figure, with a Number of very good Speakers in both Parties, and able Men of Business.

And I ought not to omit acquainting you, that it being a standing Rule to admit Members of the English Parliament to sit (tho' they do not vote) in the House among the Members, while others are only admitted into the Gallery, my Fellow-Traveller being an English Member was accordingly admitted as such, but I supposed I must have gone to the Gallery, when the Speaker having been spoken to by some of the Members, stood up and acquainted the House, that there was in Town an American Gentleman of Character, a Member or Delegate of some of the Parliaments of that Countries, who was desirous of being present at the Debates of this House; that there was a standing Rule of the House for admitting Members of the English Parliament; that he did suppose the House would consider the American Assemblies as English Parliaments; but this being the first Instance he had chosen not to give any Order in it without receiving their Directions. On the Question, the whole House gave a loud unanimous *Aye*, when two Members came to me without the Bar, where I was standing, led me in and placed me very honourably. This I am the more particular in to you, as I esteem'd it a Mark of Respect for our Country, and a Piece of Politeness in which I hope our Parliaments will not fall behind theirs, whenever an Occasion shall offer. Ireland is itself a fine Country, and Dublin a magnificent City; but the Appearances of general extreme Poverty among the lower People, are amazing: They live in wretched Hovels of Mud and Straw, are clothed in Rags, and subsist chiefly on Potatoes. Our New England Farmers of the poorest Sort, in regard to the Enjoyment of all the Comforts of Life, are Princes when compar'd to them. Such is the Effect of the Discouragements of Industry, the Non-Residence not only of Pensioners but of many original Landlords who lease their Lands in Gross to Undertakers that rack the Tenants, and fleece them Skin and all, to make Estates to themselves, while the first Rents, as well as most of the Pensions are spent out of the Country. An English Gentleman there said to me, that by what he had heard of the good Grazing in North-America, and by what he saw of the Plenty of Flaxseed imported in Ireland from thence, he could not understand why we did not rival Ireland in the Beef and Butter Trade to the West Indies, and share with it in its Linen Trade. But he was satisfy'd when I told him, that I suppos'd the Reason might be, *Our People eat Beef and Butter every Day, and wear Shirts themselves.* In short the chief Exports of Ireland seem to be pinch'd off the Backs and out of the Bellies of the miserable Inhabitants.

But Schemes are now under Consideration among the humane Gentry, to provide some Means of mending if possible their present wretched Condition. . .

The rest of the letter goes on to other topics.

Alas, Franklin's words were not prophetic. The Irish Parliament was shuttered by the British as part of the Act of Union of 1800. The poor got poorer, one million died of starvation in the Irish famine of 1847, and a million fled, mostly to America.

Franklin had merely witnessed a brief calm before an utterly disastrous storm.

CHAPTER 16

How an Obscure Irishman Built the White House but Used Slaves to Do It

Speaking at the Democratic National Convention in Philadelphia in July 2016, Michelle Obama talked about the extraordinary impact on her and her family of living in the White House as the first black family.

Referring to the White House, she stated: "I wake up every morning in a house that was built by slaves. That is the story of this country, the story that has brought me to this stage tonight, the story of generations of people who felt the lash of bondage, the shame of servitude, the sting of segregation, but who kept on striving and hoping and doing what needed to be done."

Her eloquent words summarized the journey from slavery to personhood taken by so many African Americans.

There is an overwhelming Irish aspect, too, to the story of the building of the White House. It is an extraordinary story in its own right, but burdened by the issue of slavery and the use of slaves, as was widespread back then.

It is fitting that the only known portrait of James Hoban, Irish-born architect and builder of the White House—arguably the most famous building in the world—is a wax miniature which shows him from the side with the right hand part of his face obscured.

It is as if the mystery of who James Hoban was is reflected in that shaded side with so many unanswered questions about his life and times. His embrace of slavery to the extent that he publicly bought and sold them without any moral issues whatever haunts his reputation.

Yet there is enough to write a Horatio Alger book about a penniless Irish carpenter who came to America and designed its most iconic feature, becoming the most sought-after architect in the land.

Along the way, he became a confidante of the great George Washington, who discarded all bids other than Hoban's to build the people's house, despite intense lobbying by some of the most famous architects in the world.

How did a Catholic, a peasant, and an Irishman—all marks of disdain in his times—come to beat out every major architect (not just in America but from around the world) and build and design the house that became the very symbol of America's success?

Even President John F. Kennedy, on his singular visit to Ireland in 1963, paid homage to Hoban.

Speaking before the packed parliament in the building called Leinster House, which Hoban used as the model for the White House, Kennedy said in part: "The features of this stately mansion served to . . . inspire . . . the White House. I have no doubt he [James Hoban] believed by incorporating . . . features of the Dublin style he would make it more homelike for any president of Irish descent. It was a long wait, but I appreciate his efforts."

A comprehensive new biography of Hoban, authored by White House expert Stewart McLaurin, entitled *James Hoban: Designer and Builder of The White House,* with contributions by many leading scholars, gives some new perspective on Hoban.

In the new book, it appears his links to George Washington were closer than thought and the vexed issue of slavery is given its correct weight. Those great freedom fighters Washington, Thomas Jefferson, and James Madison owned slaves and so did Hoban, who could not have finished the White House without them. Later in life, like many others, he issued a statement rejecting slavery, but there are still many questions unanswered.

We do know that the miniature of him was made in the late 1780s when Hoban, who was born in Kilkenny, Ireland in 1758, was in his early thirties. It shows a handsome young man, in looks not unlike Jefferson, with reddish hair brushed forward in the fashion of the day.

He is wearing a starched white collar and a black jacket for the sitting and the overall impression is one of urgency—a young man in a hurry.

In a hurry he certainly was: fleeing abject poverty in Ireland where he was the son of a tenant farmer, essentially a serf, on the estate of a British lord.

The tenant farmer lived on sufferance and constant fear of ejection with no rights or way to buy his own land under the rabidly anti-Catholic penal laws. The folk memory of the ethnic cleanser Oliver Cromwell, who killed off up to 20 percent of the native Catholic Irish between 1649 and 1653 in a bloody rampage through the country to extirpate papists, was still fresh. The laws he left behind were, too.

The landlord could increase the rent at any time, or throw the family out of the house with the help of the local constabulary if they saw fit. During the Irish Famine, a century later, such evictions were very common.

Hoban clearly carried the folk memories with him. He knew that his emigration was tied into those events but had moved on to the New World by the time the miniature was painted.

At the time, he was living and working in Charleston, South Carolina, where the world first encountered him in an advert placed in the Charleston and Philadelphia papers in May 1785 which advertised his services. He was twenty-seven at the time.

The ad read: "Any Gentleman who wishes to build an elegant style may hear of a person properly calculated for that purpose who can execute Joinery and carpentry business in the modern taste: apply James Hoban."

The antiquated language obscures a simple message: Carpenter for hire; if you are building a fine house, I'm your man—James Hoban.

As William Seale, American historian and White House expert, noted, it was obvious from the ad that Hoban's hands "had been dirtied" at a young age in working man's art. So this was no classically-trained top-table college graduate, but a workman who became an architectural legend through dint of his own hard work.

His memories of his impoverished childhood were clearly ones he embraced and he was known to hire fellow Irish when possible. Indeed, a rival designer, Scottish-born Collen Williamson, once complained that Hoban hired "All Irish and vagaboons to boot."

A working-class figure he may have cut, but Hoban was not without qualifications and was already a star in his native land before he departed for America.

He had been presented with the silver medal from one of Dublin's most prestigious architectural societies, a medal that would place him well in his new country and help disguise his peasant roots in status-conscious America.

Those peasant roots were deep in Irish soil. He grew up in a tenant cottage on the land of the Cuffe family. The Cuffe family's link with Ireland began during the Elizabethan times (1558–1603), when Captain John Cuffe was killed during a local insurgency. His nephew Hugh received grants of lands in both Clare and Cork for his uncle's services to the queen.

Hugh's son, Joseph, supported Cromwell in his murderous campaign in Ireland from 1649 to 1653.

It was an astute move that saw the Cuffe family gain a massive five hundred acre land grant in Kilkenny about ninety miles from Dublin. They built a Palladian-style mansion based on the works of Andrea Palladio—an Italian architect who was all the rage for a time in Ireland and Britain—to reflect their new wealth and success.

The "big house," as such mansions were called at the time by locals, was named Desart Court when it was built in 1733. It soon became the Cuffe family's seat of residence and the family eventually ended up with a peerage and a baronetcy.

It is not too tendentious to say that the White House design was influenced in part by the Cuffe mansion, which alas, no longer exists today after being burned down in 1922 as a symbol of British imperialism by the IRA after the War of Independence.

But its significance lies in its neo-Palladian design, which closely resembles Hoban's drawings of the White House.

Desart Court and the Cuffes also provided Hoban with his first opportunity to follow his boyhood dream to work on architectural design.

As the son of a tenant farmer subsisting on the estate, he easily found employment in Desart House, as his labor was very cheap.

There he trained as a carpenter and wheelwright and, having completed his apprenticeship, headed for the big city of Dublin still in his teens after securing a scholarship to the Dublin Society School of Architectural Drawing at just age fourteen.

He was arriving at a fortuitous moment—a building boom, which Hoban was delighted to learn from and eventually be a part of, was underway.

The latter half of the eighteenth century was a unique time in Dublin's history. It was fast becoming the second city of the British empire and the sixth largest, with a population of two hundred thousand in 1800, as author Finola O'Kane has written.

An expanding metropolis meant that the wealthy lived close to the Irish Sea, which became the more favored east side of the city where the gentry congregated (and do to this day); while the west side of the city was dominated by the homes of "merchants and Mechnicals" (as a 1780 book on Dublin notes).

The Dublin Society School of Architectural Drawing was a rare philanthropic institution with no fees but tough skill requirements. The mission was to teach boys of a proper age the principles of geometry and the elements of architecture. Hoban's training gave him enough skills upon graduation to practice and gave him access to an influential group of builders, architects, and craftsmen.

Hoban would have studied one of Dublin's most distinguished buildings—first known as Kildare House—which would deeply impact his design for the White House.

James FitzGerald was earl of Kildare and wished for a mansion that perpetuated his exalted status. He commissioned eminent architect Richard Castle to build his dream residence. It was built in the tradition of the grand country houses of Ireland, though it was smack in the city.

Hoban's success in convincing George Washington that the grand country house tradition was what the White House should be was based on what now has become Leinster House, home of the Irish parliament.

The White House should be lived in, not some museum artifact, he told Washington, and the great man agreed.

All this was ahead of James Hoban when, like millions before, he took the emigrant boat to America to make his career. Little did he know he would end up responsible for the most iconic building on Earth.

Hoban: The Greening of the White House

The story of how an Irish peasant's son came to America, practiced the wrong religion, and had no powerful advocates, yet ended up creating and designing the White House is akin to a tale by Horatio Alger.

In 1790, Congress passed an act creating a new city by the sea, 160 miles south of Philadelphia, the city where the business of the nation had, until then, been conducted.

In 1791, the commissioners of the new city named it Washington with the approval of the American hero who had led the independence fight.

All three branches of government—the Congress, the Supreme Court, and the executive branch headed by the elected president—would be housed within the new federal district.

Washington selected the President's House as the most important one to build first and took personal charge of the project. He did not want a palace, as he was not a king, but a dignified and impressive building and property worthy of being the stately home for American presidents. Though he was destined never to live in it himself.

Washington was sixty and an old man in a hurry. He wanted the presidential residence completed before either death or retirement stilled his voice.

French engineer Pierre Charles L'Enfant had done a remarkable job laying out the grid for the new city, but his plan for a massive mansion to be known as the President's Palace (five times the size of what was ultimately constructed) was anathema to Washington, who wanted presidents to be accessible and visible and not hidden behind palace walls.

By 1791, as he embarked on a presidential tour of the south, he clearly had the presidential residence in the forefront of his mind.

Meanwhile in Charleston, South Carolina, far from the pomp of Washington, James Hoban, the son of farming peasants who had exiled himself from Ireland, had established a name for himself as an artisan and architect.

As already noted, there was a 1775 advertisement placed by James Hoban, then twenty-seven, offering carpentry work. He had landed in Philadelphia from Ireland, but did not tarry too long there.

White House historian William Seale believes that Philadelphia was so overcrowded with builders and developers that Hoban, like many others, decided to try his luck further south.

His choice of Charleston, South Carolina at first looked strange. After all, there was a long history of anti-Irish and anti-Catholic sentiment there, and the Scots Irish who resided there in great numbers were openly hostile to Irish Catholics.

The South Carolina Assembly in 1718 banned Catholics and Irish for fears they would link up with Spanish fleets off Florida.

There was also hatred of the Catholic Church, an institution that was near and dear to Hoban's heart.

Indeed, it was not until the Civil War in 1860—when the church leader in the region, Irish-born Bishop Patrick Lynch, heartily supported the Rebels and slavery—that the acceptance of Irish Catholics came about.

By the mid-1750s, despite the ban, a smattering of Irish and Catholics were making their way south: some as indentured servants, others as displaced Nova Scotia French Catholics fleeing persecution. There was also a small number of young entrepreneurs, builders, industrialists, and land owners who came south.

Even with the addition of a small merchant class, it wasn't until 1788 that the first Catholic priest was allowed to minister in a makeshift Catholic church. In 1789, five prominent Catholics, including Hoban, acquired a space to build the first Catholic Church, called Saint Mary's. The following year, a census revealed that there were about two hundred Catholic residents in Charleston, but the number was increasing.

Hoban had another connection to Charleston that made the transition from Philadelphia a lot easier. In the late 1780s, he found himself at the front door of an Irish cousin, Pierce Purcell, a Charleston carpenter who quickly took him in and employed him at his company.

It was a home from home, as we now know Hoban had two brothers, Philip and Joseph, also living in the city and part of a coterie of young and driven Irish professionals moving south.

With Hoban as partner, and his knowledge of British and Irish architectural trends, the firm of Pierce Purcell thrived. Hoban worked on both public buildings and stately private houses, as well as public venues.

Alas, we will never know the full extent of his work in Charleston. Details about it and other parts of his life were destroyed in a fire at his residence before his death.

We do know his work included the thousand-seat Charleston Theatre and the Charleston County Courthouse.

The White House Historical Association has traced Hoban's architectural career in Charleston:

Hoban's name has been connected to public buildings and plantation houses in the Charleston area, most notably the historic Charleston County Courthouse and the William Seabrook house. A notable building in Charleston actually documented as a Hoban design was a 1200-seat theater on Savage's Green that no longer survives, though part of its foundations may still be observed at the junction of Broad and New streets. In 1790, he opened a drawing school at his new residence next door to Purcell.

Hoban was hitting his purple patch as an architect, teacher, and community leader.

By May 1791, when George Washington visited Charleston on his southern tour, the creation of the president's Washington residence was very much on his mind. Hoban was about to feel the hand of history on his shoulder.

However, Washington hardly expected to find the man he wanted in a backwater provincial city in the least glamorous part of the new country. After all, the finest architects in the land—and indeed from cosmopolitan cities like Paris and London—considered the job of building the most iconic home in the world a matter of great prestige, and they were certain to compete vigorously for the job. Indeed, even Thomas Jefferson had himself in mind to be the main architect.

The president had strict personal guidelines for his southern trek. He would never stay in homes as a guest but rather take residence in a private dwelling in order to allow him time to meet privately and also recoup his strength during his grueling tour.

For his weeklong stop in Charleston, the local leaders rented a three-story mansion owned by Thomas Heyward for Washington and his entourage. Heyward was one of four South Carolina signatories of the Declaration of Independence, and the mansion is memorialized today as the Heyward-Washington House Museum located on Church Street.

At that residence, Hoban and Washington were introduced. It was to be a fateful encounter for Hoban and America.

Washington was introduced to Hoban by city luminaries such as General William Moultrie, Jacob Rees, Henry Laurens, and, most importantly, Major Pierce Butler, who signed the Declaration of Independence and was a close ally of Washington in the victorious Revolution.

Butler and other Hoban aficionados extolled the young Irishman's talent and genius in creating magnificent buildings.

The conversation with Hoban and friends struck home with Washington. After all, he had much in common with the Irish, both having fought the British. Hoban's architectural work, not grandiose in nature but stately and distinguished, struck Washington as exactly the right kind of balance he was seeking. Most of all, he wanted a practical builder and one with whom he could get along, as he intended to be deeply enmeshed in the details.

Washington, it turned out, was a big believer in the style practiced by Irish architects. When building Mount Vernon, he described an Irish country house called Belcamp as his ideal type of residence where the "self-sufficient, modest and humble lifestyle" could be led. As Irish architectural writer Finola O'Kane noted, what Washington sought was reflected best, he felt, in Irish country houses and gardens.

Then there were the endorsements of Hoban's work. No doubt Butler's support meant the most.

Pierce Butler was born in Carlow, Ireland in 1744 into a British military family. He joined the British army, but resigned his commission to start a new life in South Carolina in 1773 with his wife Mary.

When the Revolution began, Butler, with his military training, jumped in on the rebellion side and was soon embedded in the thick of battle. He strongly distinguished himself.

The British tried to forge a southern strategy to cut off the insurrectionists there from their brethren further north. Butler was a key figure in ensuring that did not happen.

He was much pursued by Crown forces as a former Redcoat officer and had several narrow escapes from capture.

His heroism led to him representing the state at the Constitutional Convention in Philadelphia in 1787.

Alas, his embrace of slavery was total. He had gotten rich off their labors on his plantations and he was not about to endanger his holdings, especially as he suffered significant losses during the uprising.

Elected to the Senate, he authored the dreadful Fugitive Act which allowed runaway slaves to be returned to owners even from states where slavery was no more. He was elected to the Senate three times but became famous late in life once again by sheltering Aaron Burr after he killed Alexander Hamilton in their famous duel in July 1804.

At the Irish Emigration Museum in Dublin, which profiles famous Irish emigrants, the entry for Butler reads in part: "By the time of his death in 1822, Butler had become one of the nation's wealthiest individuals, and was considered one of the new republic's Founding Fathers. Yet the achievements and legacy of this particular Irish emigrant remain overshadowed by his repeated defence and advocacy of what his political contemporary, Gouverneur Morris, referred to as the 'nefarious institution' of slavery."

This, then, was the man who surely carried the most weight with Washington when Hoban was introduced to him.

Realizing Hoban had made a great impression, his partner, Pierce Purcell, shortly after made his way to Washington and inquired of the federal commissioners what the lay of the land was—literally where and how the house would be constructed. One of the commissioners remembers wryly that Purcell put forward little information about himself but lauded Hoban as the man who could do the job.

Purcell learned that an open competition was to be held with five hundred dollars for the winner and the contract to build the president's residence. Doubtless, he hightailed it back to Charleston and told Hoban to get to work. The competition to win the contract for the president's home was officially announced on March 14, 1792.

The young son of Irish peasant stock had come a long way. Now would be his greatest test. But he had a plan, one deeply rooted in his native soil. George Washington, as noted, was sixty years old and showing his age in 1792. He was also desperate to see the building of the new presidential residence and the creation of the city that would bear his name around it.

Political machinations were everywhere, especially among those denizens of Philadelphia and New York who both wanted their own cities named as the capital because of the massive economic impact of such an announcement. (New York State also offered up Kingston, a hundred miles from New York City on the Hudson, as an alternative.)

The president was besieged on all sides, and worse still, the entries he was receiving were dreadful and far from the simple stately home he envisaged.

One even had a throne room fit for a king, a title that was Washington's worst nightmare. Another entry reminded Washington of a mausoleum, while others were so grandiose that they resembled pleasure domes and palaces more than residences.

Thomas Jefferson entered secretly, but his design was rejected. England's most famous builder, Samuel McIntyre, made his bid, as did Pierre Charles L'Enfant, the French engineer who was designing the entire city at the time. All would be disappointed.

The federal commissioners tasked with coming up with a winner met religiously at Suter's Tavern in Georgetown but they were hopelessly deadlocked, much to Washington's deep chagrin.

More and more, Washington cast his mind back to the "practical builder," the Irishman James Hoban he had met during his Southern sojourn. More and more, Hoban's simple, elegant approach—as evident in his Charleston buildings—appealed to Washington.

Hoban presented two drawings personally to Washington in the autumn of 1792. With certain alterations, Washington strongly approved of one.

Though the commissioners were the men charged with judging the entries, Washington baldly interfered. As architectural expert Finola O'Kane noted: "If ever there was a rigged competition it was this one."

Washington even had Hoban address the committee and give them a letter of recommendation written by Washington himself: "I have given him this letter of introduction in order that he might have

the opportunity of communicating his views and wishes to you."
Then came the disclaimer: "I have no knowledge of the man or his
talents further than the information which I received from the gentlemen in Carolina."

But the commissioners were in no doubt as to Washington's
preference. When they made the inevitable choice, the president was
indeed pleased:

> The Plan [for the new White House] of Mr Hoban who was
> introduced to me and who appears to be a very judicious
> man was made choice of for the president's house . . . he
> has been engaged in some of the first buildings in Dublin
> —appears a master workman and has a great many hands
> [workers] of his own.

The winning design was a close facsimile of Leinster House in
Dublin, now home of the Irish parliament or Dáil.

Hoban would have been very familiar with its scope and shape,
having observed it during the years he spent training to be a builder
and architect in Dublin.

Built in 1745, in what was then the countryside, Leinster House
was the main residence of the Duke of Leinster William FitzGerald
and closely resembled what Washington wanted: a comfortable and
elegant country home rather than some monstrous palace.

Architectural writer Jackie Craven has listed the similarities
architecturally between the White House and Leinster House based
on drawings of the earliest version of the White House:

- Triangular pediment supported by four round columns
- Three windows beneath the pediment
- On each side of the pediment, four windows on each
  level
- Triangular and rounded window crowns
- Dentil moldings
- Two chimneys, one on each side of the building

Proof of the similarity was also given by Denis Bergin, director of the James Hoban Society, who wrote in the *Irish Times* in 2020 that "US historians of the White House (the three Williams—Seale, Bushong, Allman) visited or viewed Leinster House and confirmed the influence, not just in terms of external features and internal layout, but also in its exemplification of President Washington's primary brief: to have in the new federal capital a modest gentleman's residence that would blend into the country landscape he hoped to preserve in a city being built essentially on farmland."

There is no question the architectural features were very similar but the choice of Leinster House may also have been a political statement by Hoban, says White House historian William Seale.

He points out the house had also been a home for Lord Edward FitzGerald, one of the most dashing figures in Irish history, a member of the secret army known as the United Irishmen who launched a rebellion in 1798 against British rule in Ireland.

He had disposed of all his titles and worldly goods and went out to fight for Irish freedom against the British. He was greatly admired by Hoban and his Irish associates in Charleston where FitzGerald had stayed at one time. What better way to honor him than to commemorate his home and recreate it as the home of the American president, speculates Seale.

The United Irishmen, led by Theobald Wolfe Tone, were inspired by the American and French ideals and battle for liberty and equality. Lord Edward FitzGerald was by far the best known of the rebel leaders and was considered a hero in Ireland and abroad.

Abroad included Charleston where Lord Edward, in his previous life as a British officer in the revolutionary war, washed up as an injured combatant in 1781 after the Battle of Eutaw Springs.

His recuperation took place in Charleston, coincidentally in the house of a relative of George Washington.

In Charleston, despite nominally being the enemy, the handsome and flamboyant FitzGerald became a beloved figure especially among the Irish, including Hoban.

After a year recovering in Charleston, he set sail for France, where he encountered and lived with the legendary Thomas Paine, author of *The Rights of Man*, the pamphlet which became the teaching tool for revolution everywhere.

He was among the United Irishmen who convinced the French to send troops to Ireland to help kick off the insurrection. The United Irelanders sought to include Protestants, Catholics, and Dissenters in their movement as a signal of religious and political equality.

Fired with revolutionary fervor, FitzGerald was among the key figures in the insurrection but the United Irishman movement, infiltrated by spies, was doomed to failure.

He had some narrow escapes from capture, including the ransacking of Leinster House by those seeking him. Eventually, on the cusp of the Rising and thanks to informers, the British finally accosted him in his Dublin hiding place. He put up brave resistance but died from an infected wound shortly after.

He was greatly mourned. He was just thirty-four. One of the most famous songs of the era commemorates him, the duke of Leinster.

Did you see the Volunteers!
Did you see the Volunteers!
Did you see the Volunteers!
Marching to parade
Their hearts are true
Their facings blue
They are six feet high without a shoe
Did you see the Volunteers going to Parade!
  The first that in the field appears,
The first, the Dublin Volunteers,
(Let them ever be revered),
With his grace, the Duke of Leinster, His condescension ever
    kind,
His honest heart, his virtuous mind,
To Ireland's glory never blind,
His grace the Duke of Leinster!

It must have given Hoban extra satisfaction that Lord Edward, the duke of Leinster, was connected in some way to what became the White House. Hoban certainly seems to have been an Irish nationalist with strong views, no doubt a further reason for Washington, who held no brief for the British to prefer him.

* * *

The fact that Washington wanted the house built of stone added another great difficulty and also brought about the emergence of a rival to Hoban, who by this time had moved to Washington with his wife, a Maryland native. He would live there for the rest of his life.

Somehow, famed Scottish stonemason and builder Collen Williamson, who was intensely anti-Irish Catholic, was hired by the commissioners mostly because he frequented Suter's Tavern, where they held their meetings.

Acting on their instructions, he commenced building the basement of the president's house with no reference to Hoban.

He was eventually fired because of his fierce prejudice against Hoban and the Irish laborers Williamson called "vagabonds." He'd complained bitterly that Hoban favored hiring only Irish. That was certainly true.

Hoban often had problems with some hard-drinking Irish workers and he tended to deal lightly with them. His allegiance to his native country and the sons of Erin he employed was obvious.

Williamson was not the only disappointed contender who let fly publicly.

Englishman Benjamin Henry Latrobe considered himself the best architect in America. He accused Hoban essentially of plagiarism and ripping off the Leinster House design: "I feel no delicacy whatever towards Mr Hoban. If the plan of the house were his design I should be guilty of great professional impropriety but as it is acknowledged as that of the palace of the Duke of Leinster which I now have before me he cannot be offended even if he should see these remarks."

But despite enduring criticism from many quarters, Hoban had the ear of the president throughout and that was all that mattered.

There was no shovel in the ground ceremony or grand celebration, but on October 13, 1792, construction of the White House began at noon. The residence and the foundations were mostly built by slaves and African freemen, along with hundreds of Irish employed by Hoban as well as immigrants from all over. At night, after working from dawn to dusk, the slaves were locked up in nearby pens.

As superintendent of construction, Hoban oversaw everything. He became embroiled in squabbles with the federal commission which oversaw all the funding and who made life difficult for Hoban, demanding forensic accounting for every part of the construction.

Hoban knew, however, that he was Washington's man and while we do not know how often they met, there were clearly some arranged private encounters between the two men to discuss the progress.

Washington took Hoban's advice and sacked the commissioners and hired a professional oversight group versed in public buildings.

Among the most prominent was Doctor William Thornton, an eminent physician and amateur architect. He ensured that Hoban was never bothered again by outsiders.

Aqua sandstone was Washington's pick for the exterior and it was cut from a quarry located some distance upriver. Chiseling the rock was a back breaking task for slaves and free workers alike. Historian William C. Allen, who has written about James Hoban, said: "Slaves are going to do the backbreaking work. Literally, you're taking these massive rocks and coaxing them out of the earth. It's done with pick-axes and wedges. Absolutely backbreaking work."

Hoban was running a buy-and-sell slavery operation on the side. He published an ad in the *National Intelligencer and Washington Advertiser* to sell "A Valuable Strong active Negro Man" on behalf of the owner who was not "a resident of the city." Parties interested in "the terms of sale" were instructed to contact "James Hoban, who on application will make them known."

In the White House Historical Association's book, *James Hoban: Designer and Builder of the White House*, there is a paragraph that reads: "Less than a year later, Hoban placed another advertisement in the same newspaper: 'For Sale, A Negro Woman and her three Children, the eldest of whom is nine years of age, and the youngest three; the woman is about 33 years old. For further particulars enquire about Captain Hoban.'"

In 1820, according to records, the Hoban household held twenty persons, nine of whom were slaves.

Hoban did sign a petition calling for the gradual abolition of slavery, but it was too little too late.

The petition, dated March 24, 1828, called slavery "disgraceful in its character, and even more demoralizing in its influence." It noted that "people are, without their consent, torn from their homes; husband and wife are frequently separated and sold into distant parts; children are taken from their parents, without regard to the ties of nature; and the most endearing bonds of affection are broken forever."

Hoban, however, like Washington and so many, must always be viewed through the prism of their times.

Hoban's reputation as builder of the White House is untouchable but his dealings with slaves cloud him in controversy.

* * *

The entire construction took eight years and Washington never lived to see it. It was not initially known as the White House; that appellation came later. It was completed on November 1, 1800, with John Adams the first president to be installed in situ. The building was originally called the "President's Palace."

As for Hoban, he became one of the first occupants of the new city of Washington, DC, and he was in huge demand but mostly worked on government contracts. He was liked and respected. As White House expert William Seale noted: "He appeared to be easy going but was also a stickler for honest and acceptable work."

His commitment to his church never wavered, either.

The only Catholic Church near the White House was in Georgetown, too far away for many of the new congregation of Irish Catholics to attend. But in April 1794, permission was finally given to create St Patrick's Church, and the Irish in Washington finally had a religious home. Hoban eventually designed a Catholic seminary building and school to be run by the Jesuits.

In 1806, Hoban fundraised for and designed Saint Peter's Church, erecting yet another religious outlet for the city's growing number of Irish Catholics.

Hoban was highly respected and admired for his extraordinary work, both in building up the Catholic faith in Washington as well as designing the White House.

He died at the age of seventy-three on December 8, 1831. His modest obituary described him as "hospitable, generous and charitable" to all.

He became far more famous in death as the White House architect long after it became such an iconic building. His lack of earlier recognition was also due to the loss of his papers in a fire at his home, which made the historical record difficult to compile.

After Hoban's death he was interred in Mount Olivet Cemetery in Ivy City, Washington, where he and members of his family lie today. Also interred in the same cemetery is Mary Suratt, who was involved in the Lincoln assassination. The cemetery, maintained by the Archdiocese of Washington, is fully racially integrated. What Hoban opposed during his life came to be after his death.

* * *

It was not until 1901, when Theodore Roosevelt used the designation "White House" on his official presidential stationery, that the name became official.

It is now the most famous house on earth. Hoban had built a mansion for the ages, but within its walls lurks the ever-present reality of whose backs it was built on, as Michelle Obama spoke about.

CHAPTER 17

Where Did Slavery Come From in the First Place?

Where did the slave trade which tore America apart come from? While the Founding Fathers were consumed by the issue, it was not of their making.

Dr. Cassandra Newby-Alexander, professor of History at Norfolk State University in Virginia, told Aleem Maqbool of the BBC that it is a little-known fact that the United States learned the slave trade from their British masters before independence.

"Britain put its stamp on America from the beginning. It was Britain who brought the first unfree Africans to this country and helped to start slavery in America," Maqbool quotes Newby-Alexander.

The historian says the first British ships carrying slaves arrived in Old Point Comfort, in the colony of Virginia, in 1619.

"It was late August of 1619, and it was the English vessel *White Lion*," Dr. Newby-Alexander says. She believes the ship brought "20 men and women that had been ripped from their homeland in what is now Angola," said Maqbool.

Adds Dr. Newby-Alexander: "Once they were here, they [the British ship owners] began to sell those individuals that they saw as part of their cargo to the leadership in the colony."

Thus began the shameful legacy of slavery in America.

Says the professor:

America didn't officially become America until 1783 when the Treaty of Paris was signed. Up until that point, everything that America created was English, including slavery, including laws on which slavery and inequality was built. It came from England. It came from the English system.

If you claim that America has its foundational culture based on England, then you've got to take it all. That includes the systemic racism in our laws, in our practices and in our culture.

The BBC report noted that: "Policing in the southern United States had its origins in slave patrols set up under the British in the early 1700s. Local laws started to be drawn up that regarded black people as inferior."

Dr. Newby-Alexander draws a direct line to the issues America faces today: "The policing that we see that automatically assumes that a black person is a criminal, is already guilty, that started from the founding of our country that viewed Africans as systemically different."

Adds Maqbool: "A lot of the British elite again found themselves on the wrong side of history. They sent supplies and arms to the confederacy, many wanting slavery to continue because of their own business interests. Their side was defeated."

Slavery was the reason the United States almost fell apart before it was constituted. A dreadful bargain holding that slaves were not full human beings and that fugitive slaves could be returned from free states to slave states saved the Republic. If ever there was a deal with the devil, that was it.

Southern Stars

Andrew Jackson, boy soldier, and Kate Barry, fearless spy.

CHAPTER 18

The Irish Boy Soldier Named Andrew Jackson Who Fought Bravely for Washington

On February 8, 1797, an obscure congressman from Tennessee wrote directly to President George Washington seeking to influence the appointment of a new district judge in his home state.

It is the only communication ever between Washington, the imperious but beloved president, and Andrew Jackson, the hardscrabble son of penniless Irish immigrants, who would become America's seventh president and the founder of the Democratic Party.

There is no record of a reply from Washington, as no doubt hundreds of such letters were received weekly. But Washington was hardly to know that Jackson had fought heroically for the American side, even as a child, in the War of Independence and had been captured and mistreated by the British.

Washington would also never know that it was Jackson who would finally drive home for Americans how powerful and important their democratic freedom, won so nobly by Washington and his Continental Army, was to them. When the British burned the White House in 1812, it seemed a disastrous sequel could follow.

By defeating an invading British Army (which far outnumbered his troops) in New Orleans in 1815, Jackson buried the last trace of loyalism and dreams of a restored monarchy, which some still held. By so doing he gilded the memory of Washington's fight for freedom and ensured that the importance of the Revolution would never be forgotten as long as men and women walked the earth.

Jackson—"Old Hickory" to his admirers—was the original log cabin president. At his presidential library in the Hermitage in Tennessee, there is an exact replica. Of all the presidents to date, none was born poorer or with such few prospects. He was tall and thin, with piercing blue eyes and red hair. Orphaned at fourteen, his accomplishments subsequently became the stuff of legend.

He was the closest ever president to his Irish roots. His two siblings were actually born there, near Carrickfergus in County Antrim. Some have speculated he was born on the boat to America and historians agree his actual birthplace is still a matter of dispute. Both North and South Carolina claim him. Jackson himself appeared not to know. What is not in dispute is his incredible life journey.

For generations, Jackson was ranked not too far below Washington and Lincoln, a heroic man of war, a populist, and a man seen as the first "citizen president" who looked out for the little guy and took on predatory bankers.

In recent times, he has become far more controversial a figure for his treatment of native tribes and slaves, and deservedly so. It must also be noted that ten of the first twelve presidents owned slaves and many mistreated them. What is surprising is that given his own horrible experiences—as a person whose family was forced off their lands and who saw enormous hardship as a child—he was not more humane to both Native American tribes and slaves.

The family of Andrew Jackson received a cold welcome to America. What they left behind in Carrickfergus, Northern Ireland was even worse, however.

The impact of the British draconian penal laws on Ulster Presbyterians are not as well-documented as the many ways they were used to keep Catholics down, but they were severe indeed. The Crown wanted Ireland rid of Catholics and anyone else, especially

Presbyterians and Dissenters, who threatened the power and authority of the established church.

Hence, Presbyterians were denied all political power; were forced to pay tithes to the established Anglican Church; and were forced to follow the dictates of the Test Act which blocked any promotion in any field without agreeing to convert to Anglicanism. Marriages between two Presbyterians were declared void, and grants from the British treasury for Presbyterian churches were discontinued.

The Presbyterians were just as stoic as the Catholics in refusing to yield and it was hardly surprising, then, given the onslaught on their freedoms, that the emigrant ship to America was packed with Presbyterians as well as Irish Catholics. Because their ancestors had mostly come over in the plantation of Ulster in 1609 and its aftermath, when Scottish soldiers and planters were given huge tracts of land in Ireland for their service, they were known as the Scots Irish.

Among those forced to leave was Elizabeth Francis Hutchinson from Boneybefore near Carrickfergus in north County Antrim.

She was the daughter of Francis Hobart Hutchinson and Margaret Lisle of Royston, who was English-born. Later in life, she was described as "fresh looking, fair haired, very conversive."

Leaving also was her husband, Andrew Jackson Sr., who was born about 1730 in Antrim, Northern Ireland. He was listed as the son of a doctor. They were both identified as linen weavers and had been married in Carrickfergus around 1761.

Hard times, crippling tithes, and hatred for their oppressors meant that migration was the only path to any semblance of a new life.

They had two children, Hugh and Robert, and the family risked the ocean voyage and arrived in the Carolinas in 1765. They were not alone. Four of Elizabeth's sisters also made the voyage and three in-laws—James, Robert, and Joseph Crawford—also set sail for the new world. It seems like the Jackson clan upped and left en masse. They would never see Ireland again.

Their destination in the Carolina wilderness was a common one for Scots Irish settlers. Land was cheap and a community of Scots Irish expats had sprung up. A living could be made, though the presence of displaced Native American tribes made it a dangerous location. The Jacksons, however, had little choice.

The Jacksons settled on buying two hundred acres of poor land and working it. It was a site beside Twelve Mile Creek, a tributary of the Catawba River on what would today be close to the border between North and South Carolina. The area was known as the Waxhaws settlement.

Out in the Carolina wilderness they were conscious that they were isolated and alone, except for other scattered settlers. Life was dangerous, with Native American tribes frequently attacking home-steaders. The nearest big city, Charleston, South Carolina, might as well have been on the moon.

The backbreaking work was hard on Andrew Jackson Senior, and other members of his extended family seemed to have done much better at the farming trade.

Whatever the issue, Andrew's health failed and he died just three weeks before Elizabeth gave birth to future president of the United States Andrew Jackson on March 15, 1767.

Some say Jackson senior was killed by a falling tree. He was just thirty-two years old when he breathed his last, leaving a widow with two young children and a newborn she called Andrew after the father who would never see or hold him.

The odds were stacked against the fatherless little boy from a penniless, immigrant family, but even worse circumstances were to come for him.

The widow Jackson had no means of sustenance or earning, and she was forced to move in with relatives.

Jane and James Crawford had made the trip with the Jacksons to America but Jane had been stricken with a serious illness. The Crawfords requested, not entirely out of compassion, that the Jackson family come live with them in return for which Elizabeth would nurse her sick relative Jane.

"Mrs Crawford was an invalid," wrote James Parton, an early Jackson biographer, "and Mrs Jackson was permanently established in the family as housekeeper and poor relation."

Andrew spent the first thirteen years of his life in a small home as the son of the housekeeper, literally the poor relation, dependent entirely on the Crawford family's acceptance.

Elizabeth drilled a hatred of the British into her sons. She blamed the British for her family being forced to leave Ireland in the first place and she blamed them for all that had befallen her family and for the religious persecution they had endured.

Little did she know that her bitter words would be uppermost in Andrew Jackson's mind thereafter, especially at the Battle of New Orleans in 1815, where he banished the British with a hardscrabble army—defeating the men who had defeated Napoleon.

Thus, when the American Revolution began in 1776, Andrew Jackson, though not even a teenager, spurred on by his mother's stories of perfidious Albion, was desperate to fight for George Washington, as were his two brothers.

It took a few years before the battleground shifted to the south. In 1780, the British captured Charleston and flooded the Carolina countryside, robbing and beating and killing wherever they went, often assisted by Tories (Americans who sided with the British).

The war eventually reached the Waxhaws settlement with a ferocity and viciousness that confounded the people. One hundred defenders of the settlement were killed and another 150 injured in savage attacks. The bodies of many of the slain were mutilated. Amazingly, and likely to Britain's eternal regret, the Jackson family escaped unscathed.

The massacre sparked widespread outrage, as many bodies were defiled and some had suffered more than a dozen wounds. The approximately 150 wounded were placed in the Waxhaw church, where residents, including the Jackson family, tended to the wounds and administered first aid. After the Waxhaw massacre, Andrew (then aged thirteen) and his brothers, Hugh and Robert, joined a patriot regiment. Andrew became a courier.

Hugh, who had enrolled as a private, died June 20, 1779 at the Battle of Stono Ferry from heat exhaustion and wounds received.

After the Americans were defeated at the Battle of Camden, the British drove deeper and deeper into the south and a savage war of attrition began.

Andrew Jackson and his surviving brother were fugitives now as the British advanced, and the boys sought shelter in their uncle's home. The British arrived, trashed the house, and held the Jackson boys as prisoners.

The British commander then ordered Andrew to clean the mud from his soldier's boots. Young Andrew refused, stating he was a prisoner of war, and expected to be treated as such.

The commander swung his sword at Jackson, who deflected the thrust meant for his head. Jackson received two wounds as a result, and bore the scars for the rest of his life. Robert, too, was dealt a hard blow.

The Jackson boys were held as prisoners in Camden Jail, South Carolina, where smallpox was rampant. Both boys became infected with smallpox and would have likely died, but their mother, Elizabeth, arranged a prisoner transfer. Andrew walked forty miles back to Waxhaw, while his mother and his dying brother rode beside him. Robert died two days after returning home, and it was several weeks before Andrew had regained enough strength to leave his bed.

Having nursed her remaining boy back to health, Elizabeth went to Charleston where several members of the Crawford clan were being held in horrific conditions aboard a prison ship.

Soon Elizabeth herself fell ill and died in November 1781 at Charleston, helping the sick to her last days.

Andrew was now alone in the world. He blamed the British for sweeping his mother and brothers away.

Later in life he wrote about his mother, saying she "visited that City [Charleston] with several matrons to afford relief to our prisoners with the British—not her son as you suppose, for at that time my two Elder brothers were no more; but two of her Nephews, William and Joseph Crawford, Sons of James Crawford, then deceased. I well recollect one of the matrons that went with her was Mrs. Barton. If possible, Mrs. Barton can inform me where she was buried so that I can find her grave. This to me would be great satisfaction, that I might collect her bones and inter them with that of my father and brothers."

Andrew Jackson's father and brothers were laid to rest in the Old Waxhaw Presbyterian Church cemetery near Jackson's birthplace.

As for his Irish mother, Jackson continued to seek her last resting place.

Mrs. Barton (A woman who attended his mother on her deathbed) was interviewed and she remembered that when Elizabeth Jackson contracted her fatal disease she had been nursed in Mrs. Barton's home.

After her death, Barton dressed Elizabeth in her own best dress and buried her in an unmarked grave. Not until 1949 was a plaque to her erected at the Waxhaw grave where Elizabeth's husband and two sons lay.

From such unpromising beginnings, Andrew Jackson performed the extraordinary feat of winning the presidency. His victory at New Orleans consolidated democracy in America and would surely have gladdened Washington's heart.

On the down side, his treatment of slaves and Native Americans has undermined his historical record forever, much as it has undermined many of the early presidents.

* * *

The son of Irish immigrants fought for Washington and secured Washington's historic legacy forever. Like Washington, he was first in battle and first in the minds of men.

He understood the value of democracy.

In his inaugural address in 1829, he stated: "As long as our government is administered for the good of the people, and is regulated by their will; as long as it secures to us the rights of person and of property, liberty of conscience, and of the press, it will be worth defending."

He had heard about the oppression his family went through in Ireland. He saw, firsthand, how the British Crown could only rule by brute force in his own country.

Ironically, although of Scots Irish descent, he became unpopular among many Irish Protestants because he allowed Irish Catholics to enter America in large numbers. Jackson, who died in 1845, made it clear that religious freedom meant freedom to worship in whatever faith.

Jackson profoundly changed America. Every president up to 1824, bar John Adams, was an elite slave-holder from Virginia. Jackson, the fighting Irishman from nowhere changed who could become president forever.

In the history of America, few did more to consolidate and build on Washington's legacy than the flinty, fearless, and fearsome Andrew Jackson, a true son of the Scots Irish Diaspora.

CHAPTER 19

The World Turns Upside Down as Kate Barry Becomes Southern Paul Revere

The South Carolina Encyclopedia states that Kate Barry, who was to become one of the south's great heroes in the Revolutionary War, was born "Margaret Catherine Moore in County Antrim, Ireland, the daughter of Charles and Mary Moore."

However, other sources place her as born in South Carolina in November 1752, shortly after her parents arrived there from Ireland.

We do know, according to the encyclopedia, that her father received a land grant of 550 acres near Spartanburg in South Carolina, which eventually became the Walnut Grove plantation in Spartanburg. Today, it is a landmark heritage site as the birthplace of Kate Barry.

It is difficult to get completely accurate information on the life of Kate Barry. One of the major books is a fictionalized biography which is of little value as a reliable document, and she clearly fell victim to a degree of male bias with the major spotlight shining on the men of war.

Kate and her family were typical of the landowners that gathered in the Carolinas after fleeing persecution from the Anglican Church in Ireland because of their Presbyterian faith. She was one of ten siblings, children of Charles and Mary Moore, and the family worked long hours on the upkeep of the estate. They also employed about ten slaves.

Not too far from where Kate's family farmed, the family of future president Andrew Jackson also established a homestead after fleeing Northern Ireland.

The Revolutionary War theater had shifted south after the British defeat at Saratoga in 1777 and a major attempt to subjugate the South began, the plan being to conquer the South and then move north.

The war in the South was much more a civil war, with settlers choosing sides and being pitted neighbor against neighbor. It was characterized by viciousness and levels of atrocities seldom seen elsewhere.

The British were initially successful in seizing Savannah and eventually Charleston and pushed deep into settler territory in an attempt to kill off the South and advance north where matters were at a stalemate.

Kate Barry, born in the saddle, and married at fifteen to militia captain Andrew Barry, became a masterful scout as the British advanced—tracking enemy movements, riding the Native American trails, and crossing swollen rivers in pursuit of enemy troops and their location.

On one of those scouting missions, she discovered a large detachment of the British advancing on Spartanburg, unbeknown to her husband Andrew's militia or to the regular army.

In a desperate dash to save them, she tied her two-year-old to the bedpost in her home before galloping off to rouse the Patriots, Paul Revere-style, alerting them just in time and saving countless lives.

On another occasion, so the story goes, she is said to have been captured but refused to divulge any information to her interrogator who flung her to the ground.

Another famous intervention appears to have happened at the Battle of the Cowpens on January 17, 1781, when Henry Morgan's elite southern troops faced the might of the British Army, led now by Lord Cornwallis.

George Washington had astutely named one of his best generals, Nathanael Greene, as his southern commander. Greene did what no commander should do—he split his army, forcing Lord Cornwallis to do the same.

Colonel Henry Morgan, a hero of Saratoga, took command of half the rebel army and was now engaging Lieutenant Colonel Banastre Tarleton. Tarleton was a deeply controversial character accused of ordering the slaying of Patriot soldiers in previous conflicts even though they had surrendered.

Again, it is said that Barry was a key figure in monitoring the British advance. Morgan had sent out an urgent plea for spies and scouts and she was foremost among them. As a woman, she was able to get closer than other scouts to pinpoint Tarleton's location, while arousing less suspicion.

As for the battle itself, Henry Morgan proved to be just as astute and brilliant a tactician as he had been at the Battle of Saratoga.

He held his army together on what looked like unfavorable terrain. Wide open fields ideal for British dragoons and a swollen river behind his army which meant they could not retreat, as some had done, to avoid bayonet charges,

The Cowpens itself was a five hundred yard field where cattle grazed at certain times of the year.

The two armies faced each other across the field to the skirl of Scottish bagpipes from the British Highland regiment. Initially, it seemed to be swinging the British way until Morgan's cavalry—led by George Washington's cousin, William Washington—entered the fray in decisive fashion. At the same time, the Patriot infantry charged.

The battle lasted less than an hour and ended in complete victory for Morgan. The British losses were huge: 110 dead, more than two hundred wounded, and five hundred captured. Morgan lost only twelve men with sixty wounded.

There is a direct line between the Battle of the Cowpens and the ultimate British defeat at Yorktown.

Cornwallis knew any hope of holding the South had vanished and the British sought to fight their way back to Virginia. However, the Patriot army was waiting at Yorktown. The British eventually surrendered, and the world turned upside down.

Once again, Barry had played her role in ensuring vital intelligence about the movement of the army was relayed back to the Patriot side. She proved her courage and helped Morgan to give the British, in his words, "a devil of a whipping."

Today, she is remembered in South Carolina at the Citadel Military College. As mentioned, her homestead is also a national landmark. There is a Barry County in Georgia named for her, as well as a portrait of her hanging in the Georgia State Capitol.

Like Paul Revere's iconic midnight journey, her dashing ride to warn of the British arrival has gone down in poetry and in history. When she passed away in 1823, the daughter of Irish immigrants received a hero's send-off.

It was well deserved. She was a true star of the South.

The Rogue's Gallery

The Irish general who tried to replace Washington, the Irish sergeant hanged for treason, and the ex-con who dreamt up his greatest scheme which involved Washington in an Irish jail.

CHAPTER 20

"The Conway Cabal"—A Rogue Irish General Seeks to Overthrow Washington

George Washington atop his white steed dashing into battle and turning near defeat into victory at Yorktown is one of the great images every schoolchild absorbs when learning about the Revolutionary War.

What is rarely discussed in school is the role of the "Conway Cabal," a group led by an audacious Irishman. Thomas Conway was convinced Washington was a terrible general and had to be replaced.

That an Irish immigrant would lead the attempt to bring down Washington, the only concerted effort of the war among plotters on his own side, is surprising indeed.

Yet, in the context of the times, it is hardly surprising that there was hostility to Washington. The early part of the war went very poorly and there will always be naysayers. History is full of polemics about what poor soldiers General Ulysses S. Grant or Douglas MacArthur were, in the Civil War and Korean War respectively.

Washington was the first and only president to directly take part in an uprising. Questioning leadership was a part of the burgeoning democratic process in America, even when those accusations were leveled at the father of the country.

Every culture and country has its foundation myths and George Washington not telling a lie—absurd as it seems—was part of his godlike profile. Likewise, his reputation as a flawless general was a convenient fable.

But the man himself was wonderfully mortal despite the alabaster statue figure he would become. Forever framed on dollar bills as a sixty-three-year-old tired and toothless old leader is the iconic painting of him by Gilbert Stuart (who was determined to paint the definitive portrait even while languishing in an Irish debtors' prison and who we will learn more about later in this book).

That human condition of fallibility extended to the field of battle, where Washington often made mistakes.

A major one was trying to stop the onward tide of Redcoats on Long Island as they came ashore and marched toward New York City. Halting them would prove an impossible task that should never have been attempted, as he later admitted.

The concept of Washington's invincibility is shattered when one takes a closer look at the seventeen battles he fought: he won seven, lost seven, and three were undecided. Two of the major battles lost were for New York City and Philadelphia. The Continental Army was barely clinging on, and the critics began to murmur that it was the fault of the commander rather than the brave fighting men.

The 1777 Philadelphia defeat, particularly, caused an eruption of doubt in the Continental Congress that Washington was up to the task. Suddenly, the prospect of victory against the British dimmed and a whispering campaign began against the leader of the Revolution. It threatened to become a full revolt.

The attempted coup was led by an extraordinary Irish-born character named Thomas Conway, who had served in the Irish Wild Geese units of the French Army before offering his services to Washington.

Born into a wealthy family in Cloghane, Kerry, in 1733, Conway, as were so many others, was deeply afflicted by the Penal Laws which essentially denied education to Catholics in an attempt to stamp out the Papish religion in Ireland.

Like other Catholics of means, the entire family moved to France to have their children educated in the faith of their forefathers. His father and grandfather had served in the Irish Wild Geese units of the French Army. By December 1747, aged only fourteen, he himself was named as a second lieutenant in the Irish Wild Geese regiment and he fought in the Seven Years War, defending the port of Cherbourg from British invasion. The Seven Years War between the French and the British, from 1756 to 1763, was fought over who would secure the upper hand in Europe and essentially the known world.

Conway progressed through the ranks until being made a colonel in 1772.

He viewed the looming war in America as an opportunity for him. An ambitious man, he saw service with the Americans as a passport to greater rank when he returned to France.

In 1776, he arranged a meeting with Silas Deane, one of the American plenipotentiaries in Paris at the time. Deane furnished him with a letter of introduction that ensured him a senior rank in the Continental Army and rapid promotion. On December 14, 1776, Deane's letter in hand, he departed from France and set sail for America.

Once he had arrived he was quickly ushered into the ranks. He would prove a highly controversial figure.

In an article for *Journal of the American Revolution*, Andrew Zellers-Frederick writes: "Many historians have described Conway as authoritative and derisive. On occasions, he refused to obey orders that he disputed. Altogether a most ambitious and self-proclaimed military genius, he was always judgmental of both those above him in rank and of subordinates."

He thought of Washington as a mere amateur and felt the commander-in-chief held a grudge against him because of his criticisms.

Washington certainly denied him promotion, even though Conway could lead and he could fight, as he proved at the Battle of Germantown when he commanded Washington's right flank and played a decisive role in the victory.

Conway stated openly that Washington's failures at New York and Philadelphia called for a new leader and he gathered a group of prominent individuals around him.

They also had a likely replacement for Washington, the British-born General Horatio Gates, who had stopped the British Army in its tracks twice at Saratoga in upstate New York as it marched south seeking to cut off New England from the rest of the Patriot army.

Gates had turned the tide at the two battles of Saratoga, though most historians now believe it was future turncoat Benedict Arnold who led from the front on the first battle who secured the victory.

Gates, never a man known for self-effacing modesty, had made it clear he was available if Washington continued to founder.

Born in Malden, England, Gates left the British Army and immigrated to West Virginia in 1772 and soon identified with the Patriot side, chafing at the colonial control of the country.

In 1775, he was named adjutant general of the Continental Army and in 1777 he took over the Northern battalions of the army.

His victories in Saratoga, where the British general Lord William Howe surrendered suddenly, launched dissident hopes that Gates was the perfect candidate to replace Washington.

Historians have long debated how much Gates knew about the plot and how deeply in it he was involved.

Influential figures flocked to his standard, many from New England who felt ignored by the Washington leadership.

Among them was the eminent doctor Benjamin Rush who wrote: "I have heard several Officers who have served under General Gates compare his Army to a well regulated family. The same Gentlemen have compared Genl. Washington's imitation of an Army to an unformed mob." (Rush later tore all pages critical of Washington out of his famous work *Travels Through Life*.)

There were also those fearful of Washington having too much power at the time, including Sam Adams and John Adams, the latter fearing Washington was turning into a demi-god.

Conway decided to act, gauging the dissident numbers sufficient to do so. His letter to Gates called Washington "a weak general" and stated providence had brought Gates along at just the right time.

But Washington had excellent internal intelligence sources and received a copy of Conway's letter via a loyal courier. John Fitzgerald, Washington's Irish-born chief aide, carried out a secret investigation and reported back to Washington on those involved. Washington acted quickly. He wrote to Gates:

> I am to inform you then, that Colo. Wilkenson, in his way to Congress in the Month of October last, fell in with Lord Stirling who inform'd his Aide-de-camp Majr McWilliams that Genl Conway had written thus to you "Heaven has been determined to save your Country; or a weak General and bad Counsellors would have ruined it."

Conway was caught red-handed and desperately tried to flatter Washington and make him doubt his own eyes.

Conway called Washington "a Brave man, an honest man, a patriot, and a Man of great sense." He continued that his "modesty" was such "that although your advice in council is commonly sound and proper, you have often been influenc'd by men who Were not equal to you in point of experience, Knowledge or judgment." He claimed that he could "attest that the expression *Weak General* has not slipped from" his pen.

Gates went even further in his own reply to Washington by asking him about the letter and vainly protesting it was all bunkum: "His [Conway's] Letter was perfectly harmless, howeve'r, now that various Reports have been circulated concerning its Contents, they ought not to be Submitted to the Solemn Inspection of even those who Stand most high in the Public Esteem."

No one in Washington's inner circle was buying the humbug from Gates or Conway. Founding Father Alexander Hamilton upbraided Conway. Tench Tilghman, Washington's aide-de-camp and close confidant, slammed Conway by stating: "He has come down full of his own importance and wrote the General [Washington] a letter for which he deserved to be kicked. He [Washington] treated it with the contempt it deserved."

General Nathanael Greene stated that: "A horrid faction has been forming to ruin his excellency and others. Ambition, how boundless! Ingratitude, how prevalent! But the faction are universally condemned."

Washington had long had suspicions, as Andrew Zeller-Frederick wrote in *Journal of the American Revolution*:

> From the beginning, Washington was not totally oblivious to the actions of Conway and his confederates. He stated that "there was a scheme of this sort on foot last fall admits of no doubt but it originated in another quarter—with three men who wanted to aggrandize themselves—but finding no support, on the contrary, that their conduct, and views when seen into, was like to undergo severe reprehension they slunk back—disavowed the measure, & professed themselves my warmest admirers."

Conway resigned from the army but Washington's supporters never forgot the scheming Irishman who had tried to undermine America's greatest hero.

Conway was a marked man, considered a traitor by some, even after the war had concluded.

Conway challenged Brigadier General Cadwalader, a close ally of Washington, to a duel for scathing comments made about him. Cadwalader's bullet hit home as a contemporary account outlines: "At a distance of 12 paces he [Cadwalader] fired and Shot Conway thro the side of the face, on which he fell & was carried off the field. He is supposedly not to be in danger unless unforeseen inflammation should produce it."

Many anti-Conway Patriots thought the shot fired by Cadwalader truly found its proper mark in Conway's mouth.

Conway however, thought he was dying and he made an abject apology to Washington:

> I find myself just able to hold the pen. During a few Minutes, and take this opportunity of expressing my sincere grief of having Done, Written, or said anything Disagreeable to your excellency. My career will soon be over, therefore justice and truth prompt me to Declare my Last sentiments. You are in my eyes the great and the good Man. May You Long enjoy the Love, Veneration, and Esteem of these states whose Libertys [sic] your Virtues. With the greatest respect sir your Excellency's Most obedt humble servant.

But Conway did not die; he recovered and returned to France where he was reinstated in the army with the rank of brigadier general.

He later became a colonel stationed in Hindustad, India, and went on to receive several promotions including governor general of French-held areas in the Cape of Good Hope region. But his health began to fail, no doubt aggravated by the dueling injury. His cousin, Robin Conway, wrote: "General Conway is now at Bath [an English town famous for its healing baths] for his health." He further commented that: "He was in a fair way of making money but General Conway is such a man that spends a deal of money and nobody knows how; he owed, I am told, on his return to Europe 70 thousand Livres. His Brother is much more prudent and much a better Country Man."

Conway's leadership style was dictatorial. A local trader wrote: "This man is insofar as anxious, violent, and awful, inasmuch as our General has never been the right one to run the colony . . . The hope is that another heart failure will free us from that man."

Back in France in 1790, as revolution stirred, Conway took the royalist side and led secret organizations sworn to uphold monarchy.

As with Washington, his conspiracy was uncovered and when the trial of Louis XVI began, a *memoire*—signed by Conway and setting out his tasks to protect the monarchy—was uncovered.

Conway fled to London where, in yet another twist, he was named commander of one of the Irish brigades in the British Army. He even got the opportunity to kiss the king and queen's hands upon his appointment, as one report noted.

But his bad health meant he never actually led his troops into battle and he died on March 3, 1795. He was remembered by his British Army colleagues with full military honors despite having fought against them most of his life—leading to speculation he might have been on their payroll all along, which would explain the "Conway Cabal."

To this day, debate rages over the Conway Cabal and how serious a threat it was to Washington.

Leading historian John C. Fitzpatrick believed it was very serious due to Washington's naiveté:

> Its seems incredible that Washington could have been the center of such a hideously selfish and unpatriotic coil without knowing more about it, yet it is perfectly in keeping with the high sense of honor in the man that, without any evidence beyond that of the jealous and intriguing dispositions of Gates and the rest, he suspected nothing beyond the boundaries set by their personal ambitions.

Yet Washington must have known, particularly after Chief Aide John Fitzgerald laid it out for him.

* * *

Conway kept in touch with his Kerry heritage.

He was known amongst his friends as "Old Colonel James," and a distinguished officer of the French Army. That he was quite a veteran in the French service is evident from a letter dated February 13, 1767.

In the letter (discovered by familysearch.org) he wrote in 1767, forty years after he left Ireland, he addressed relative Robert

Fitzgerald, M. P. for Dingle and afterwards Knight of Kerry. Conway discussed his ambition and outlined his desire to secure "a post as Commander of some of the Troops permanently stationed on the Coasts of France, to guard them, or else some similar employment of a quiet honorable kind which would afford a retreat from a more active life." He added that "this ought not to be difficult to obtain for a man who has served for 40 years past."

Served *who* might be the most pertinent question.

CHAPTER 21

Washington Hangs an Irishman— Traitor or Fall Guy?

On June 20, 1776, a crowd of twenty thousand, most of them Continental Army soldiers, gathered near the Bowery in New York to witness the first public execution of an American soldier for treason.

Sergeant Thomas Hickey from Ireland was hanged as a traitor after being found guilty in a court martial of mutiny, sedition, and conspiracy following the discovery of a plot to kill George Washington.

The army was present in full regalia at the express wish of Washington who wanted to make an example of Hickey as to what would happen to traitors in their ranks.

Thomas Hickey was described as "a dark-complexioned man of five feet six, well set . . . an Irishman and hitherto a deserter from the British Army." It was the largest crowd, likely before or since, to witness the hanging of a man, little consolation for the Irishman with his head in the noose.

But Hickey was not just any soldier. He was a member of the Life Guards, in essence Washington's Secret Service detail, and is said to have been a personal favorite of Washington, which made his betrayal all the more hurtful to the commander in chief.

But that was not the full story. Hickey was by no means the leader of the attempt to assassinate Washington, and was little more than a useful idiot in the eyes of many. The real perpetrators, including prominent loyalists New York Governor William Tryon and New York Mayor David Mathews, would never be prosecuted.

Indeed, forty suspects would be arrested in dawn raids but only Hickey was convicted. Among those released was Mary Smith, then housekeeper for Washington, an example of how close the conspirators were to getting the rebel leader.

At Hickey's court martial, a fellow soldier named William Green admitted to recruiting Hickey for the plotters but, seemingly, was never charged.

Hickey had joined the British Army and fought bravely in the Seven Years War between Britain and France. He later fought in America with the British in the French and Indian War. He rose to become personal aide to British general Sir William Johnson, also Irish-born, but once Johnson departed for England Hickey lost his access to power.

When the Revolutionary War began, he soon defected to the other side, not an uncommon occurrence, as loyalties were not as firm as they would become later on in the war.

The Patriot leaders found him an invaluable recruit because of his British Army training and background, and he was soon chosen for the elite Life Guards.

It was a time of great intrigue. Just a few months prior, an extraordinary maneuver by George Washington had resulted in the surrender of the British in Boston. Washington's men, led by Colonel Henry Knox, son of Irish immigrants, had, in the dead of winter, dragged powerful cannons from upstate New York to the heights overlooking Boston.

There, the high ground gave Washington's army full sight of the exposed British defenses and ships which could not swivel their guns to challenge them.

Soon, the British recognized the hopelessness of their position and surrendered in return for safe passage. The rebels the British had been so contemptuous of were far more resourceful than they gave them credit for.

The victory had cemented Washington's almost mystical reputation even more. Those around him were worried, however, that he had come to embody the American Revolution so much that he was an obvious target for assassination.

The formation of the Life Guards was a move to try and protect the commander-in-chief.

The word went out to all units to send a few of their best men to form the new force, and Sergeant Hickey, British Army-trained and well-versed in war and protecting senior officers, was an obvious pick.

The note from Washington's office was clear, only the best men were needed:

> The General is desirous of selecting a particular number of men as a guard for himself and baggage. The Colonel or Commanding Officer of each of the established regiments, the artillery and riflemen excepted, will furnish him with four, that the number of wanted may be chosen out of them. His Excellency depends upon the Colonels for good men, such as they can recommend for their sobriety, honesty and good behavior. He wishes them to be from five feet eight inches to five feet ten inches, handsomely and well made, and as there is nothing in his eyes more desirable than cleanliness in a soldier, he desires that particular attention be made in the choice of such men as are clean and spruce.

The Life Guards stood watch outside Washington's quarters day and night and accompanied him—parting crowds, pushing well-wishers back—alert for assassins and always on the lookout for other dangers. All in all, it was very similar work to the role of the Secret Service today.

Hickey was deeply trusted, often taking the prime position of directly standing guard outside of Washington's domicile whether it was at Valley Forge where the army wintered or a townhouse in New York City.

The commander-in-chief did not lack for enemies. After leaving Boston in triumph and taking control of New York, Washington faced a hornet's nest of disaffected loyalists, all of whom had lost power because of his hegemony over the city.

No loyalist was more put out than Governor William Tryon. He was forced to flee to a ship offshore, called the *Duchess of Gordon*, under guard by a Royal Navy ship where he commenced his plot to kill or capture Washington and disrupt the city's defenses.

Tryon was full of love for his colonial masters as he had just come from a year in Britain where he apparently received an audience with the king and came home flush with devotion to the monarchy and all it stood for.

A parade to welcome him back soured him even more. Washington, by coincidence, arrived from Boston the same day and led a triumphant march down Broadway. Tryon's parade was puny by comparison. There would be no truck with Washington.

New York Mayor David Mathews was in a similar pickle. As mayor, he enjoyed rich pickings from city contracts and outright bribes. Suddenly, the Washington administration was dismissing him as unimportant because of his loyalist lean. He had become a nobody.

While Tryon and Mathews plotted, Washington desperately tried to stiffen New York's defenses against the incoming British assault. With the British fleet only a few weeks away it was an impossible task.

Tryon and Mathews plotted on Tryon's ship. They became excited at the notion of delivering a gift for the king and crown by killing or capturing Washington. Both men dreamed of past glories returning. That would not take long with the British back in charge.

There was fertile ground for turncoats. Soldiers were badly paid, worked like dogs building fortifications, and were definitely aware that Washington did not have even a row boat or vessel of any kind to take on the mighty British Navy. When that navy armada arrived, onlookers counted 160 ships.

Tryon recruited men to go into Patriot areas and seek out turncoats by promising funds and lands when the British arrived if they turned on their fellow soldiers and created mass confusion.

The project was led by a gun maker called Gilbert Forbes who had been secretly providing weapons to Tryon and other loyalists and who was brought into the plot with promises of money and land.

The plot unfolded thus. Forbes would visit pubs such as Lowry's, Corbies, and Chauncey's Tavern (still open to this day) and recruit Continental soldiers.

Showing the desperate state of affairs Forbes soon lined up sixty turncoat soldiers, among them Sergeant Hickey and an Englishman called William Green, both from the president's own security detail.

What caused Hickey to turn on Washington? Money and greed seemed the obvious answer. The wages for the Continental Army had been delayed by months. Hickey was probably broke and desperate. A Loyalist offering ten sovereigns and possibly free land after Washington was captured or killed surely found a willing ear in Hickey who had previously shown he had no qualms about deserting.

The modus operandi was that each man was approached in a public or private place at the recommendation of a member and asked if he wanted to make some serious money. If he agreed, a swearing-in was conducted in a grand mansion by David Mathews, mayor of New York. Each man then became a member of the conspiracy and made more money than they imagined, with more to come when the British reached New York and started the offensive.

It seemed only a matter of time. Washington supporters knew the plot against their boss was thickening, but even using specially-created counter-intelligence groups they could not locate the loyalist cell.

Then Hickey made a fatal mistake.

He and a fellow Irishman and co-plotter Michael Lynch were arrested trying to use counterfeit bills, likely in a dimly lit tavern, a very common practice at the time.

Thrown in Bridewell jail, they had a third companion in the cell, one Isaac Ketchum from Long Island; held coincidentally also due to counterfeit money practices along with three other suspects from Long Island.

Ketchum had no particular politics but when Hickey and Lynch tried to interest him in joining the conspiracy he decided to play along.

He was a widower with six children and had played by far the smallest part in the Long Island counterfeit effort.

Suddenly, he saw a way to freedom as the two Irishmen blabbed on about killing Washington, seizing bridges, and recruiting soldiers. He wrote a note to the warden saying he had urgent news and asking to speak to the highest legal authority in the city.

Amazingly, his request was granted and Ketchum told the authorities, headed by no less a figure than John Jay, future chief justice of the Supreme Court, the outline of the plot, which is how Hickey was busted and arrested and the entire scheme to kill Washington fell apart. It turned out to be just in time as the 160 British ships had appeared over the horizon and soldiers aboard were ready to come ashore at any time.

Some of the conspirators revealed the role of the New York mayor. Mathews was thrown in jail but soon after he mysteriously disappeared. Tryon, who was untouchable, continued to live on board the *Duchess of Gordon*, protected by a British warship.

In the end, following dawn raids, more than sixty names of turncoats, spies, malcontents, and top officials such as Tryon and Matthews were named in the scheme by the investigating body.

But only Hickey got the noose.

Why that was is a matter of speculation. The most likely answer is that revealing the scheme in full and showing how many were prepared to switch sides would have damaged morale among the Patriot soldiers on the eve of battle.

In addition, many—such as Mathews—were civilians and would have had to go through a much different and lengthier legal process than Hickey who could be court-martialed quickly.

And so it proved. At his court martial Hickey tried to say it was all a clever plot by him to infiltrate the opposition but no one was buying it.

Ketchum's testimony sealed the deal. "In different conversations he informed me that the Army was becoming damnably corrupted," Ketchum told the court-martial that tried Hickey. "That the fleet was soon expected; and that he and a number of others were in a band to turn against the American Army when the King's troops should arrive." The verdict was death by hanging.

Washington wanted it done right away and issued a statement to that effect.

Hickey had the noose tied over his head, but why were the others allowed to get away?

The historian David Ellis told author Brad Meltzer much of the assassination ring story is still hidden history centuries later.

George Washington's inner circle tried to make sure there was no record of their actions. Meltzer recalls talking to Ellis during the course of his research for his book (co-written with Josh Mensch), *The First Conspiracy: The Secret Plot to Kill George Washington.*

Said Meltzer: "We were dealing with a story that was about spies. [Ellis] said, 'You can find the number of slaves at Mount Vernon. You'll never find all his spies. By its nature . . . this is something that will always be elusive.'"

Washington likely won the war because of his spies. A prison spy had saved his life, as well.

A witness to the hanging, which took place in a park located near the Bowery District, was army surgeon and future Massachusetts Governor William Eustis.

Writing to a colleague, Eustis called the Hickey conspiracy "the greatest and vilest attempt ever made against our country . . . the plot, the infernal plot which has been contrived by our enemies."

Eustis described Hickey's last moments: "At 11 the prisoner accompanied by the Provost Master and Chaplain and a Guard of 80 men with bayonets fixed took up the march from the brick guard house to the place of executioner's which was a tree."

Eustis reported that: "Hickey appeared unaffected and obstinate to the last except when the chaplain took him by the hand under the gallows and bade him adieu. A torrent of tears flowed over his face but with an indignant scornful air he wiped them with his hand from his face."

Sergeant Hickey went to his death bravely, not hesitating when the noose was placed around his neck. His last words were to hope that his accomplice Green, his fellow officer who recruited him but got away, would face the same justice he did. Then the hangman sprung the hatch door.

The fates of fellow Life Guards—drummer Green, Johnson (a fifer), and privates Lynch and Narnek—were markedly different. All got off. Hickey in the end was a scapegoat for those higher up, all the way to Governor Tryon, who'd attempted to have Washington killed or captured.

* * *

Washington made his statement right after the trap door opened, no doubt in stentorian tones:

> The unhappy fate of Thomas Hickey, executed this day for mutiny, sedition, and treachery, the General hopes will be a warning to every soldier in the Army to avoid those crimes, and all others, so disgraceful to the character of a soldier, and pernicious to his country, whose pay he receives and bread he eats. And in order to avoid those crimes, the most certain method is to keep out of the temptation of them, and particularly to avoid lewd women, who, by the dying confession of this poor criminal, first led him into practices which ended in an untimely and ignominious death.

Thus died the first ever traitor in the American army.

CHAPTER 22

How Gilbert Stuart Escaped an Irish Prison to Create One of the Most Famous Paintings in History

In 1789, George Washington was elected the first president of the United States by sixty-nine electoral college votes to zero, an extraordinary victory.

The pomp and heraldry and huzzahs greeting the extraordinary victory could be heard across the new land.

Three thousand miles away, in a debtor's prison in Dublin, lay Gilbert Stuart, a painter of great renown but low morals, whose attempted flight from his Irish creditors had landed him in jail.

Yet, even as he languished in a lonely Irish cell, the news of Washington's ascent to the presidency sparked an idea so audacious that, if it worked, could be the making of him.

The new president would be his unwitting accomplice in a grand scheme to win his freedom and make his fortune.

You could hardly picture two men with more different lives. They couldn't have had less in common. Not even their politics were shared, as Stuart was a royalist who had fled America to Britain and later Ireland when the revolution happened.

But somehow, a few years later, they would make history together, and join forces to create something that reverberates to the present day—something with which every American born ever since is intimately familiar. James Flexner, writing in *American Heritage* magazine in 1976, on the two hundredth anniversary of the American Revolution, rightfully called that event deeply historic.

He was referring to Gilbert Stuart's painting of a grim faced and tired sixty-three-year-old General George Washington—one of the most famous paintings in the world.

Flexner wrote:

> The face is familiar. Every American has scanned it a thousand times; it passes from hand to hand in millions of ordinary business transactions every day of the year. It is Gilbert Stuart's image of George Washington, and it adorns, of course, the United States dollar bill. Yet not one American in a hundred could tell you anything of the artist whose perception of the Father of His Country would eventually become the most readily recognized portrait ever made of any famous person.

The 1796 image is perhaps the best known in the world—carved into Mount Rushmore and framing so many historical artifacts from buildings to public places to the very capital of the United States itself. It is known as the Athenæum portrait because it was on display in the Boston Athenæum library.

The truth about the painting by Gilbert Stuart, who was born in 1755, is very surprising and it comes with a very close connection to Ireland where they claim him as one of their own. Despite only spending a handful of years in the country, he was included in Walter G. Strickland's highly regarded *A Dictionary of Irish Artists*, published in two volumes in 1913.

While in Ireland for a period of six years from 1787 to 1793, he also won a reputation as a dissolute and drunken carouser and became known for ripping off many who posed for portraits, including some of the most important and prominent men in Irish public life.

As Washington biographer Ron Chernow noted, Stuart was "overly fond of liquor, prodigal in his spending habits, and with a giant brood of children to support . . . "

He faced grave problems in 1789 as an unwilling inmate of Marshalsea Prison, effectively a debtor's prison in Dublin Ireland, near where the current Four Courts, the center of the Irish legal system, is based.

Drunk and dissolute he may have been, but there is no question the man was a genius portrait maker at a time when it was considered one of the great high art professions.

Before Ireland, he had fled to London from New York after taking the Redcoat side in the Revolutionary War.

Evidence of his skill is given by William Templeton Franklin, grandson of Benjamin (to many Americans the greatest of the Founding Fathers), who wrote to his grandfather rather excitedly from London:

> I am afraid you will think me tedious in returning home—and I begin to think so myself, and can assure you I have no Desire of staying longer here, and I should in all probability have got away this Week, had not my Father express'd a great Desire that I would sit to Stewart, who is esteem'd by West and everybody, the first Portrait Painter now living: he is moreover an American: I have seen several of his Performances, which appear'd to me very great indeed! He is astonishing for likeness's. I heard West say—"that he *nails* the Face to the Canvass."—by which he meant I believe to express, not only that the Resemblance of the Person was perfect—but that his colouring did not change; a fault common to some of the first Painters in this Country—and particularly to Sir Joshua.
>
> I am to begin sitting tomorrow, and Stewart has promised to make all possible Dispatch. He hopes to finish the Principal Parts by Monday; if so, the Day following I shall endeavour to get away, provided I can in the mean time make another Visit to your good Friends Mr. and Mrs. Sargent.

The artist, however, also became almost as well-known in England for his alcohol excess and being constantly in debt, which led him to flee to Ireland.

Once there, he tried in vain to convince the Irish gentry that he was a follower and relative of the Royal House of Stuarts and was of Bonnie Prince Charlie's royal lineage, but few believed him.

What he was in the British vernacular was a "cad" who left unpaid bills. One of his famous ruses was to start a portrait, receive half the payment, and then bolt.

When he was sober and so minded, much of what he did were actually superb portraits of famous figures.

Stuart's genius was that the sitter invariably liked the portrait, no easy accomplishment.

Art historian Carrie Rebora Barratt, formerly of the Metropolitan Museum of Art, writing in a 2003 essay about Stuart, stated:

> He knew well the conventions of portraiture, easily rendered the attributes of gentility and affluence, and succeeded time and again in executing portraits that fulfilled in pictorial terms the wishes and desires of his sitters. That said, he maintained that his success had little to do with a sitter's character or accomplishments, but rather more with his own artistic abilities. More than once, Stuart escorted to his studio door sitters who thought otherwise.

Such encomiums were common in his day, and Stuart soon attracted a hard-drinking, admiring crowd in Ireland who loved to imbibe with him.

Stuart's daughter Jane admitted in correspondence that her father utterly enjoyed the convivial atmosphere, the high spirits, and the nightlong parties the Irish held—but his long-suffering wife felt much different.

Jane, his twelfth child and a fine portrait painter in her own right, who died in 1888, wrote three articles about her father in *Scribner's Magazine* in 1886 and 1887.

She recalled that her father was delighted with "the society he met in Ireland. The elegant manners, the wit and the hospitality of the upper-class Irish suited his genial temperament." She concluded: "I am sorry to say Stuart entered too much into these convivialities." She also wrote that she never could get her mother to discourse much upon the experiences of these days, as "it gave her pain to remember anything associated with his reckless extravagance, or what she called his folly."

She added: "Those interested in further details may consult Dunlap or Herbert." She was referring to John Dunlop, his personal unofficial biographer, and William Herbert, an Irish painter he befriended—the twin sources of most of the stories regarding Stuart's stay in Ireland.

At first, Stuart thrived in Ireland. After just a year, he had become the painter of choice of major ecclesiastical figures, and he made a good enough living painting bishops and deans and anyone else in their pomp. He painted John Fowler, archbishop of Dublin, and William Bennett, bishop of Cork, as well as many political figures, too.

He resided in the village of Stillorgan outside Dublin, by no means a tony address, but debtors can't be choosers.

His financial finagling soon became known to authorities, especially when the subjects of paintings found, to their chagrin, that only half of their canvas was in oils and the rest missing. In many cases he had promised a painting of a major figure would be ready, but it was not.

Stuart upset enough powerful people that he found himself in debtors' prison. Not that debtors' prison was a hell-hole, at least not for the well-connected. Writing a century later, an inmate of Marshalsea remembered the rather spiffing time he'd had behind bars:

> I remember the Marshalsea Prison in Dublin, and in that gaol we had a nice suite of rooms, and we had balls there, and many a pleasant hour I have spent there, in the society

of many of the most delightful men in Dublin, who were in the habit of spending some time at that resort. This was 25 years ago, and it was perfectly well recognised then that there was no kind of punishment in the debtors' gaol. They were held there until they made an arrangement with their creditors, but they had everything that their means would allow them to have in prison.

The problem for Stuart was that he had no means and was outside the charmed circle. Desperate to escape, he set about his grand plan.

It involved a very fanciful scenario. First, he would have to escape from prison, then find some passage aboard a ship from Ireland to America and once there, gain access to the rock star of the era, the greatest general of all, George Washington, and paint his definitive portrait.

It was not absolute madness, though. After all, in an age where news took weeks to arrive, little was known in America about Stuart's Irish misadventure and his reputation as a portrait painter was still white hot. He also had the gift of the gab like all good conmen, and he was certain he could access Washington if he could only get to America.

His intention was to go back to the land of his birth and seek out Washington. Then, ensconced in the president's residence in Philadelphia, he would paint Washington's portrait.

* * *

He told friends in Dublin he intended to go to America: "There I expect to make a fortune by Washington alone. I calculate upon making a plurality of his portraits, whole lengths, that will enable me to realize; and if I should be fortunate, I will repay my English and Irish creditors."

Stuart was uninterested in Washington the military hero, in fact, but he saw Washington as his meal ticket out of poverty.

As he wrote, he saw the president "as a resource to rescue myself from pecuniary embarrassment, and to provide for a numerous family at the close of an anxious life, I have counted upon the emoluments that might arise from a portrait of George Washington, engraved by an artist of talent."

Incredibly, his plan worked. Firstly, there was the little matter of breaking out of jail. Stuart said afterward that his escape from Marshalsea Prison was aided by guards whose portraits he had painted in an especially flattering light. At a time before photography, a painting of oneself was a rich reward for a prison guard and certainly worth looking the other way for as a prisoner escaped over the prison wall, which is precisely what Stuart did.

Stuart fled Ireland, leaving dozens of paintings unfinished. He told a friend: "The artists of Dublin will get employed in finishing them . . . the likeness is there and the finishing may be better than I should have made it."

Thus, unencumbered by his fraud and free under the most extraordinary circumstances, Stuart arrived in America as a man with a plan.

Washington's name was on every lip, yet a visual rendering had not been made that caught the public imagination.

Stuart was about to change all that.

Ron Chernow has written about how Stuart mapped out his path to Washington with the "precision of a military campaign."

He inveigled himself into the company of the family of Chief Justice John Jay and had him sit for a magnificent portrait which flattered the first chief justice no end.

Soon, he had his letter of introduction to Washington and the sittings were approved by Mrs. Martha Washington.

Finally, he was in the august presence of the greatest American hero. But the body chemistry was wrong. Stuart, feckless and talkative, soon annoyed the aloof Washington who had little time for tittle tattle. Stuart was disheveled in dress; Washington was always perfectly attired. Try as Stuart might, he could not enliven or engage the stone-faced Washington.

Besides, it wasn't the young and dashing leader of the Revolution the artist was capturing. Washington was sixty-three when Stuart met him and the years of war and incredible mental and physical strain had left their mark, not least the loss of all or most of his teeth, a fact he tried to conceal.

Art expert John Hill Morgan wrote: "People lose sight of the fact, or do not know, that Stuart never saw Washington until he was sixty-three years old, and after he had lost his teeth, which circumstance entirely changed the shape of his face and his expression as well."

Hill Morgan stated Washington was feeling the years—his giant frame was breaking down, as a result of his long public service, and he was old beyond his years.

Morgan wrote that people refused to believe that Washington looked at any time throughout his life other than as Stuart represented him. The younger, more vigorous George Washington simply did not exist. Perhaps, they wanted to see him as father of the country in an older, fatherly pose.

Those who knew Washington at the time of Stuart's paintings were in no doubt that the old rogue had pulled off his greatest masterpiece.

Writer and art expert John Neal said: "If Washington should return to life and stand side by side with this portrait and not resemble it, he would be called an imposter." Stuart had pulled off the impossible, vaulting to freedom from Irish debtors' prison and somehow fulfilling his ambition to paint the definitive portrait of Washington, the most famous American of all time.

He painted five presidents in all, but only one became the coin of the realm—his portrait of Washington as familiar today as it was back then.

He went from a debtors' prison in Ireland to the very highest levels in his profession. Stuart never resolved his financial issues and would die deeply in debt in 1828, with an estate valued at just $375. Today his work is considered extraordinary, meriting permanent exhibition at the New York Metropolitan Museum.

Meanwhile, billions have seen, touched, and felt his portrait of Washington. It is an extraordinary tribute to Stuart, the down-at-heel alcoholic, whose daring escape from an Irish prison made it all possible.

Washington's Family Celebrated Irish Links for Generations

Irish support during the Revolutionary War was taken very seriously in the Washington household and was never forgotten. It was celebrated well beyond Washington's death.

Although he had no children himself, Washington adopted those of his widowed wife, Martha, and raised them as his own.

George Washington Parke Custis, Washington's adopted grandchild, held the cause of Irish independence particularly dear. He may have been the author of one of the most famous Washington lines on Ireland but some historians say Washington himself uttered it: "When our friendless standards were first unfurled, who were the strangers who first mustered around our staff, Erin's generous sons. Ireland, thou friend of my country in my most friendless day."

Custis counted Saint Patrick's Day with Washington's Birthday and the Fourth of July as the three "holidays" he celebrated.

He demanded in his will that fresh shamrock be placed at his grave every Saint Patrick's Day. Starting in 1956, the Irish in Washington honored his request.

As the *Washington Post* reported on March 18, 1989, the celebrations, which also involved the Irish Embassy, were heartfelt:

Since 1956, Washington's Irish have gathered on St Patrick's Day at the house George Washington Parke Custis built, near the place where he is buried, to honor his memory and abide by his wish that the Irish place a shamrock on his grave. If you'd lived in the District in the 1840s, you would have likely heard of Custis, adopted grandson of George Washington and father-in-law of Robert E. Lee.

Custis—a farmer, painter, orator, patriot and great supporter of Irish independence—presided over an annual St. Patrick's banquet in downtown Washington.

Agnes Mullins, a historian, employee of the National Park Service, and curator of Custis's home, Arlington House, told the *Washington Post*:

> Custis would go down to Alexandria, rent a boat, gather up all the Irish he could find, fly a green flag with a golden harp and sail up the river to the 14th Street wharf. Upon arrival, Custis and his guests would be greeted by hordes of merry-makers. They would all parade up 14th Street to Carusi's Salon, where the party would continue.

It is clear from those accounts recorded seventy years or so after the Revolution that the Irish role had not been forgotten by the Washington family, and the extent of the debt owed by America continued to be recognized by America's first First Family. That fact ensured the Irish of the Revolutionary War found their own pursuit of happiness to be by Washington's side defeating the British.

For the Irish, who were devoted to Washington and his cause of defeating the hated British, the clear gratitude and affection shown by the Washington family was deeply appreciated. Erin's green standard bearers were proud to stand with the stars and stripes.

INDEX